Designing Websites

according to
the Ancient Science of Directions

Designing Websites

according to
the Ancient Science of Directions

Dr. Smita Jain Narang

A Sterling Paperback

STERLING PAPERBACKS
An imprint of
Sterling Publishers (P) Ltd.
A-59, Okhla Industrial Area, Phase-II,
New Delhi-110020.
Tel: 26387070, 26386209; Fax: 91-11-26383788
E-mail: sterlingpublishers@airtelbroadband.in
ghai@nde.vsnl.net.in
www.sterlingpublishers.com

Designing Websites
according to the Ancient Science of Directions
© 2006, *Dr. Smita Jain Narang*
ISBN 81-207-3071-3

All rights are reserved.
No part of this publication may be reproduced, stored in a retrieval system or transmitted, in any form or by any means, mechanical, photocopying, recording or otherwise, without prior written permission of the author.

Printed and Published by Sterling Publishers Pvt. Ltd., New Delhi-110020.

णमोकार महामंत्र

एसो पंच णमोक्कारो सव्व पावप्पणासणो।
मंगलांण च सव्वेसिं पढमं हवई मंगल।।

I bow my head to almighty, with whose grace and blessing I have been able to write this book.

Dedicated to

My parents
Mr. Shikhar Chand Jain *&* **Mrs. Keemti Jain,**
who have given me the best virtues inc life and who always believe in me.

My husband
Mr. Raj Narang,
The strength of my life and a constant source of inspiration who has given me his precious guidance at each and every step and without whom my dream of fusing the two sciences would never have come true.

Acknowledgement

I would like to thank Mr. Dinesh Agarwal, CEO, Indiamart Intermesh Ltd and Mr. Brijesh Agarwal, COO, Indiamart Intermesh Ltd. for providing me with all the sites and data relating to them.

I would also like to thank Mr. Naveen Gupta for always guiding and providing me with all the knowledge of Astrology.

I want to thank Mr. & Mrs. Gopal Sharda who have always been the guiding spirit in my life and also to my best friend Sona Sood who has always boosted my confidence.

My deep gratitude and sincere thanks goes to my in-laws, relatives and friends whose moral support was extremely valuable to me during the writing of this book.

I would like to give a special thanks to my publisher Mr. S.K.Ghai, for his guidance and interactive communication.

$\mathcal{P}$REFACE

Man has endeavoured to improve from time immemorial. Starting from the Stone Age to the 21st century, mankind has only improved and is keeping its step toward modernisation. But as we are becoming modern we are leaving our culture far behind and are overburdened by sorrows, unhappiness, mental tensions and what not. Thus all kinds of sufferings are taking place in the life and in order to get all the good things back, we are trying to follow the path showed by our ancestors.

Vastu is a complete science and based on the principles and logics, has been formulated by our saints thousands of years ago. We are simply using those fundamentals to make this world a better place to live with peace and happiness.

The "sick building syndrome" has made us aware of the toxic effects of many interior elements. Ergonomics has made us aware of furniture, which can help to avoid strain and injury. So I want to formulate the logical principles for the most hot topic of today, "The Internet". What I have in mind is that when the principles are the same, then why cant we use it for the construction of websites, its just implementing the principles and formulating some new logics.

From rooms to Net, Vastu has it all; this is a truth. Vastu is not merely designating the rooms or placing the objects, it is basically the path that takes us to the destination of peace, prosperity and happiness.

In my book I have tried to formulate some principles for designing the websites on the fundamentals of Vastu science, so that the person can achieve the maximum benefit in totality.

I have started this book because I was keen to find an answer that when the visiting cards, letter heads, marriage cards can be designed according to Vastu then why can't the websites. I started searching myself and became confident when I saw that my predictions were correct. Then I started this research very seriously. The points and comments given here are my own views and my own perception.

In the book, I have tried to correlate the three major sciences, that is the Vastu science, the science of astrology and the computer science. I have tired to show that the fusion of Vedic concepts with modern system can be very beneficial for the mankind.

A website is the image of a person's attitude, his perception and about his business too and Vastu is the science of orientation that combines all the five elements of nature and balances them with man and materials.

The main motive of doing this research is to fuse the two different sciences, the modern computer science and the Vedic Vastu science. The new generation thinks that to be a computer wizard is the best they can achieve in life, and some discard our own traditions, our Vedic culture. So, I want to make them realise that this modern science is also based on our ancient Vastu science.

1. To bring into focus the essential features of Vastu Shastra and the underlying meaning of their principles and to bring them into practice for benefiting the mankind.
2. To explain that how the ancient scientific principles of Vastu can be combined with today's most modern science, the computer science.
3. To enlighten the new generation for whom 'Net' is the advance technology and "Culture" is the orthodox, that this modern science is also based on our ancient precious culture and is governed by the principles formulated by our saints and sages.

To share the knowledge and experience I have gained doing this research with all other people so that they can be benefited and our old ancient culture "the Vastu science" can be applied with modern technology.

The world comprises of five basic elements, also known as the *panchbhootas*. They are **earth, water, air, fire** and **space**. Out of the nine planets, our planet has life because of the presence of these five elements. Similarly, I have tried to prove that every website has five elements and any disturbance in any of these established elements can cause an imbalance in the site that effects the website business adversely.

I am only trying to smoothen the people business by making it more harmonious and thereby having gradual increase through websites. Destiny always prevails, but by implementing the Vastu concepts, one can enhance the business provided by websites. Therefore, it is advisable to follow Vastu to open the gates to a happy and prosperous life.

The objective of doing this book:

1. The main motive of doing this book is to fuse the two different science, the modern computer science and the Vedic Vastu science. The new generation think that to be a computer wizard is the best they can achieve in life and discard our own traditions, our Vedic culture. So, I want to make them realise that this modern science is also based on our ancient Vastu science.
2. To bring into focus the essential features of Vastu Shastra and underlying the meaning of their principles and to bring into practise for benefiting the mankind.
3. To explain that how the ancient scientific principles of Vastu can be combined with todays' computer science.
4. To enlighten the coming generation for whom Net is the life and culture is the death, that this modern science is also based on our ancient precious culture and is governed by the principles formulated by our saints and sages.

In this book, efforts have also been directed towards finding a common link between websites, Vastu science and astrology. This type of correlation serves its purpose in overcoming the unscientific fear. Faith and intellect are not two poles apart, but in fact are two sides of the same mind.

Dr. Smita Jain Narang

www.webvastu.com
www.vaastu-shastra.com
smita@webvastu.com

Contents

Dedication		*vii*
Acknowledgement		*ix*
Preface		*xi*

1. **Vastu Shastra–An overview** — 1
    - 1.1. What is Vastu Shastra?
    - 1.2. Origin of Vastu Shastra
    - 1.3. The Five Elements
    - 1.4. The Directions
    - 1.5. The Mandalas
    - 1.6. The Shape
    - 1.7. The Open Space around the Building
    - 1.8. The Proportions
    - 1.9. The Projections
    - 1.10. The Retractions
    - 1.11. The Basic Vastu Principles
    - 1.12. The Doors
2. **The Ancient and Scientific Approach to Vastu Shastra** — 17
    - 2.1. The Ancient Approach
    - 2.2. The Scientific Approach

2.3. The Magnetic Field
2.4. The Solar Radiation

3. **A Deep Study of Internet**   24
    3.1. What is Internet?
    3.2. How Internet Came into Being?
    3.3. A Brief History of Internet
    3.4. The Beginning
        ❖ Communication
        ❖ Business
        ❖ Education
        ❖ Information
        ❖ Entertainment
        ❖ Humanity Considerations
        ❖ Sharing Data

4. **Extensive Study of the Websites**   43
    4.1. Designing the Website
    4.2. Initiating the Website

5. **Introduction to Web Vastu**   48
    5.1. The Five Elements of Web Vastu
    5.2. The Orientation
    5.3. Why North?
    5.4. The Shape
    5.5. The Graphic Mandalas
    5.6. Analysis according to Web Vastu

6. **Research on the Proposed Layout:**
   The Earth Element   66
   - 6.1. What is Layout?
   - 6.2. The Layout
   - 6.3. Layout according to Vastu Shastra

7. **Research on the Proposed Fonts/Graphics:**
   The Water Element   71
   - 7.1. What are Fonts?
   - 7.2. What are Graphics?
   - 7.3. Types of Typefaces
   - 7.4. How to Choose the Typeface/Graphics?
   - 7.5. The Typography
   - 7.6. The Guidelines for Designing fonts
   - 7.7. Basic Outlines
   - 7.8. Fonts As Per Vastu
   - 7.9. Graphics As Per Vastu

8. **Research on the Proposed HTML:**
   The AIR Element   81
   - 8.1. What is HTML?
   - 8.2. HTML Flags
   - 8.3. HTML according to Vastu Shastra

9. **Research on the Proposed Colours:**
   The Fire Element   91
   - 9.1. What is Colour?
   - 9.2. The Colour Theory

- 9.3. The Colour Wheel
- 9.4. Behaviour of Colour
- 9.5. Colour Scheme
- 9.6. Colour Symbolism
- 9.7. Colour Significance
- 9.8. Colour for the Web
- 9.9. Colours According to Vastu

10. Research on the Proposed Names: The Space Element — **106**
- 10.1. What is Name?
- 10.2. Hunting a Name
- 10.3. Name for the Website
- 10.4. Name according to Vastu Shastra

11. The Time Factor — **112**
- 11.1. Uttrayan and Dakhiyanan
- 11.2. The Shapes of the Moon

12. Case Studies — **117**

Bibliography — **134**

1   Vastu Shastra – An Overview

Vastu is the science of direction that combines all the five elements of nature and balances them with man and materials. It is all about the interaction of various forms of best effect on a living person. It aims to create a subtle conducive atmosphere in a structure in which we can bring the best in ourselves, thereby paving the way for enhanced health, wealth, prosperity and happiness in an enlightened environment. Like any other science, Vastu is universal, rational, practical and utilitarian. It is not a religion but a science.

Vastu is a very deep and ancient science of directions and if someone starts writing on Vastu, there is no end. But here only those basic principles are discussed on which the website designing is based.

The Vastu Principles

1.1 What is Vastu Shastra?

Vastu means abode or a house and Shastra means science or technology, i.e., it is the scientific method of house construction. Vastu Shastra considers a house to be a living soul, having prana. And therefore, this science in a way defines the relationship between man and the cosmos. Indian civilisation is considered as one of the oldest in the world and hence Vastu Shastra. In the Vedic period, people used to construct homes, temples and hermitages with a view to have peace and harmony in life. But, in todays' world we are building concrete jungle, mainly for the high rate of return. This blind race to make buildings not in accordance with the ancient bye laws of nature has led the world into pollution, environment and ecological problems with no peace of mind under any kind of shelter.

Vastu is an inherent energy concept of science. We cannot see energy with our naked eyes but we can realise and see its application in different forms and fashions. We all know that "upto the knowledge of mind is called science and beyond the knowledge of mind is called spirituality." Hence, Vastu is not only a science, but is a bridge between man and nature, thus teaching us the art of living.

The principles laid down in Vastu Shastra were formulated keeping in view, the cosmic influence of the sun, its light and heat, solar energy, directions of wind, the moon's position, the earth's magnetic field and the influence of cosmos on our planet. The system is an admixture of science of directions, astronomy and astrology.

Vastu principles are geological, geometrical, geophysical, botanical and above all cosmological and celestial in nature. The aim of the Vedic philosophy was to discover first, the secret laws of the universe and then from them to shape a pattern of everyday life. Vastu is a very ancient science and is essentially that art of correct settings whereby one can place him in such a manner so as to absorb the maximum benefits of the *paanchbootas* as well as the influence of the magnetic field surrounding the earth. The scientific use of the elements creates a perfectly balanced environment, which ensures enhanced health, wealth and prosperity.

> *"We owe a lot to the Indians, who taught us how to count, without which no worthwhile scientific discovery could have been made."*
> *–Albert Einstein*

Our sages and seers knew the secrets of using all the five elements of this universe and their special characteristics and influences. They evolved scientific methods and systems and confined them over the years as 'Vastu Shastra'. Our sages searched it; we are only researching it and building the concepts.

Vastu Shastra works on three principles of design that cover the entire premise. The first one is *bhogadyam*, which states that the designed premises must be useful and practical in approach. The second is *sukha darsham*, in which the designed premises must be pleasing to eyes in accordance with aesthetics. The third principle is *ramya*, where the designed premise should be beneficial for the user and should be a part of its well-being.

1.2 Origin of Vastu Shastra

Vastu shastra found its origin in *Stapatya Veda*, which is part of *Atharva Veda*, one of the four Vedas. About 5000 years ago, Vastu science was followed intensely during the Mahabharat Era, as described in our Vedas and Upanishads. During this era, a demon named Maya was a pioneer in architecture, wrote a book called *Maya-Mahatamya*, which is still available. Vishwakarma was also a pioneer who constructed Dwarka city. About 21,65,095 years ago, Lord Rama had used Vastu science at many places. There are various texts on the subject like – *Brihat Samhita, Kashyap Shilpa Shastra, Vishvakarma Vastu, MayaVastu, Mayamatam, Matsyapurana, Samaraanagana Sutradhaar* and many more.

Samaraanagana Sutradhaar optly asserts:

Sukham Dhanaani Budhischa Santhathi Sarvadhaanrunam
Priyaaneyshaam Cha Samsiddhee Sarvamsyathu Subhalakshanam
Yatra Nindhit Lakshmathra Thahee-The-Sham-Vidhath Krith

Atha Sarvamupadeyam Yadveth Subhalakshanam
Desah pur Nivasas cha Sabhaveesma Sannaanicha
Yadhya Dheedhrusa-many-as acha Thatha shreyskaram matham
Vastu Shasthraa Dhruthe-tasya Na syal-laksanananirnaya:
Thasmath Lokasya Krupaya Saathametha-dhurir yathe

The essence of this elegant shloka is that a well planned house as per Vastu Shastra will give all pleasures, wealth, intelligent children, peace and happiness, redeem one from debts etc. Disregard to Vastu will result in unwanted travels, bad name, grief and disappointments. All houses, villages, towns and cities should be built conforming to Vastu Shastra. Vastu Shastra, is therefore, ushered in for the betterment and overall welfare of the people in this world.

From ancient literature, we gather that Vastu was treated as the science of construction of temples and royal palaces. In *Amarakosa*, a Sanskrit dictionary written by Amara Simha and epics like *Skanda Purana, Agni Purana, Garuda Purana* and *Vishnu Purana*, the principles pertaining to the science of Vastu had been enunciated. Apart from these works, epics like the *Bruhatsamhita, Vishnu Dharmottara Purana, Viswakarma Vastu Sastra, Samarangana Sutra Dharana* and *Aparajita Prutchcha*, have been responsible for Vastu taking shape as a science. The first official treatise on Vastu, the *Kasyapa Silpa*, has been attributed to Sage Kasyapa. In the treatise *Agama Sastra*, which explains the science of temples, Vastu is considered as the basis for any type of construction. Excavations at Harappa and Mohenjodaro also indicate the influence of Vastu on the Indus Valley Civilisation.

Vastu is based on the interplay of various forces of nature involving the five elements – earth, water, air, fire and space and strives to maintain equilibrium as these elements influence, guide and change the lifestyles of not only human beings but every living/non-living character on earth.

1.3 The Five Elements

Out of the nine planets, our planet has life because of the presence of these five elements. The world comprises five basic elements, also known as the *paanchbhootas*. They are earth, water, air, fire and space. Earth and water have limited and

Air		Water
	Space	
Earth		Fire

localised availability for the human habitat and growth. We address our almighty as *Bhagvan* which is again comprises five elements where *Bh* (Bha) stands for Bhumi (Earth); *g* (ga) 'for gagan (Space); *v* (va) for vayu (Air); *a* (aa) for agni (Fire) and *n* (an) for neer (water).

These five elements reside in the nature in a specific predetermined proportion and are governed by the principles of creation, which are beyond human understanding. A study about these five elements becomes necessary to understand the science of Vastu in its true spirit.

1.3.1 EARTH (Bhumi)

Earth, the third planet in order from the Sun, is a big magnet with North and South poles as centre of attractions. Its magnetic field and gravitational force has telling effects on everything on the earth – living and non-living. It comprises the land structure, landform, landscape, flora and fauna. It takes everything in itself; this is the base of all the life. Scientists have established that the earth was formed 460 crores years ago. Originally it was a fiery ball but due to melting of the rocks, the surface of the earth has been formed. It gradually drifted away from the orbit of the sun and got cooled and solidified.

Billions of years ago the atmosphere comprising dust particles began to shrink into a globe due to the reciprocal gravitational pull among the particles. The globe started rotating around itself and got spilt into various fragments in course of time. During this process 90% of the mass remained static while 10% started encircling the static mass in an elliptical orbit. The static mass became the Sun and the revolving mass took the shape of nine planets. According to the scientific theories, earth is a mammoth magnet, which has acquired magnetism due to magnetic particles embedded in it. It has two poles, North Pole and South Pole. The southern pole of this magnet is located in the Northern Hemisphere and the northern pole in the Southern Hemisphere. Based on the magnetic principles, the distribution of load is done in Vastu Shastra.

1.3.2 WATER (Jal)

This is represented by rain, river, sea and is in the form of  liquid, solid (ice) and gas (steam, cloud). The thick hot gases surrounding the earth gradually got cooled off and formed clouds, they gave rainfall and the water flowed in the low-lying areas and water bodies were formed.

We get water in three forms, liquid (water), solid(ice) and gas(vapour). The ice melts with the heat of the sun, forms liquid, the water. The water gets evaporated, forms clouds which then bring water in the form of rains. Thus this is a natural cycle.

It forms part of every plant and animal. Our blood is nothing but water with haemoglobin and oxygen. The habitat and physical life are where water is present. This is true for all life forms and eco-cultures. The type, form and pattern of life also greatly depend on the relationship of earth and water. If we see our history, all the cultures had developed on the banks of water bodies. This shows the influence of water on our lives, since ages.

1.3.3 AIR (Vaayu)

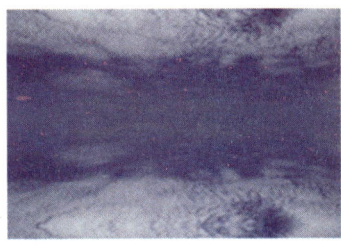

Air envelops the earth in motion. As a life-supporting element, air is a very powerful life source. Pure air with oxygen is good for brain and blood. Atmosphere of earth which is about 400 kms, in depth, has oxygen, nitrogen, carbondioxide, helium, other gases, dust particles, humidity and vapour in certain proportions. Human physical comfort values are directly and sensitively dependent on correct humidity, airflow, and temperature of air, air pressure, air composition and its content. In this aspect, air deals with the entire body surface through skin, blood system and through respiration. Air also represents the movement.

1.3.4 FIRE (Surya)

The whole atmosphere has been compressed into the shape of the globe by the reciprocal gravitational pull of the atoms scattered all over. Due to the friction between atoms, heat is generated and it pervades throughout the universe. Our sun is a mammoth star and the thermonuclear reaction in the sun produces heat and light. Earth derives heat and light from the sun. Sun represents light and heat without which the life will extinct.

All the days and nights, seasons, energy, enthusiasm, passion, vigour is because of light and heat only. Sun is a source of mental energy too. Best minds evolve in a natural process where the sun is temperate. Not very hot, not very cold, just the right temperature of 24 degrees. The different zones with the variety of climate have distinctive culture and architecture. Sun has played an important role in the development of visual qualities of architecture in terms of textures, colours and above all the expressions of vitality.

1.3.5 SPACE (Aakash)

Sky is an endless space. The entire universe exists in this vacant space. All the above elements are skilfully engineered towards the creation of physically comfortable, emotionally pleasant, intellectually determinant, totally vibrant and blissfully  satisfying spaces for human shelter and habitat. It is an unending region remote from the earth, in which not only our solar system but the entire galaxy exists. Its effective forces are light, heat, gravitational force waves, magnetic field and others. It is an endless entity. Space is the result of big bang theory, which stated that universe was full of an explosive material twenty lakh crore years ago. A big explosion had caused the material mass to disintegrate and scatter into four directions. These fragments are called Milky ways, each milky way is composed of dust and gasses besides innumerable stars. Our solar system is located at the end of one such milky way.

1.4 The Directions (Orientation)

The importance of orientation of a building is not only for saving energy but also to have a better healthy house design, which not only gives a comfortable living but also gives good health, prosperity and wealth to the house owners/occupiers and their families. There lies a co-relation between the rotational scenario of the planets and the house design and their different directions with respect to North. The building of any type and its construction meets the purpose if proper orientation has been given using suitable local building material. It increases not only its life span but also improves the condition of the occupants. There are instances where buildings, not planned according to required local orientation are lost or deteriorated much faster than the buildings having built with proper studies of orientation.

The proper orientation means the proper knowledge of all the eight directions. It is a common knowledge that the direction from where the sun rises is known as East (*poorva*) and where it sets as West (*Paschim*) and when one faces the East direction, towards one's left is North (*uttara*) and towards one's right is South (*dakshina*). The corner where two directions meet obviously is more significant since it combines the forces emanating from both the directions. According to Shastras if we worship, revere and respect the Lords of these eight directions, they will shower on us their blessings and benefits. Let us examine their importance according to scriptures.

NORTH: This is a place of Lord Kuber, the god of wealth. Planet Jupiter represents this.

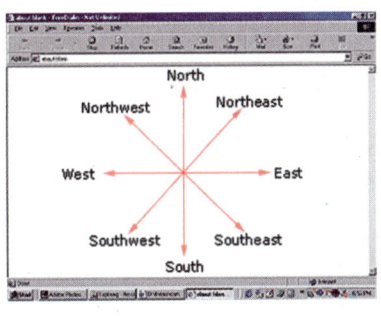

NORTH- EAST: This is a place for Lord Eeshaan, this is a source of health, wealth and prosperity. He grants us wisdom, knowledge and *serve mangla*, and relieves us from all sufferings. This is governed by planet Mercury.

EAST: This is governed by Lord Inder and he is the king of devaas. He gives wealth and all the pleasures of life. It is represented by the planet Venus. The East is where it all begins in Vastu Shastra.

SOUTH - EAST: This is the place for the lord of fire – the agni. He gives us the good personality and all the best of life. It is a source of health as it is related to fire, cooking and food. It is governed by the planet Moon.

SOUTH: This is a place of Yama, the god of death. He is embodiment of dharma, and eradicates all evils and grants all good things. This represents the planet Mars.

SOUTH - WEST: This is a place for Niruti, the god who protects us from evil or enemies. It is a source of character, behaviour, case of longevity and death. Planet Rahu or the dragon's head governs this.

WEST: This is a place for Lord Varun, the lord of rains. He showers his blessings through rain and brings prosperity and pleasure in life all around. This is represented by the planet Saturn.

NORTH - WEST: This is a place for Lord Vayu, he bestows on us long life, health and strength. He is the basic of all life. It is also a source of change in course of business, friendship and enmity. It is governed by Ketu, the Dragon's tail.

BRAHAMSTHAAN: The brahmasthaan is the open space and is represented by Lord Surya and the Planet Sun.

The element in each quadrant must be honoured and they should be kept in balance as this creates powerful and beneficial conditions, which draw business towards the owner. To avoid the calamities caused by not following the principles of Vastu and assure all round prosperity and happiness, our sages and saints showed the way by unfolding the secrets of Shastras.

Profounding the principles and practices of Vastu Shastra which is in perfect harmony with the nature and in consideration of our aesthetic needs, architectural requirements, astrology and other aspects of Earth sciences.

1.5 The Mandalas

The ancient sages were aware of the hidden force underlying the universe and used symbols and myth both to describe it and as a means of reconnecting to the invisible world. In the *Mundaka Upanishad*, it is described as that which is neither tangible nor antecedent. Colour, eyes, ears, hands, feet; of that which is prevalent everywhere, immeasurably minute, self-evident, indestructible, always alive.

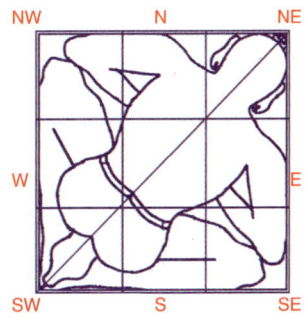

The idea is not far from modern physics. One of the fundamental laws of physics is that matter equals energy. Science now proclaims that the universe started as energy and transformed into matter, and that forms consist of tightly bound energy. To understand Vastu, one should understand the *Vastupurusha Mandala*.

5.1.1 Vastupurusha Mandala

Purusha and *mandala* are associated with Vastu (site). Vastu encompasses the house with the site and its environment. This mandala is based on the sacred square, a symbol of the cosmos, and it shows the relationship of the elements to the cardinal points. The *Vastupurusha Mandala* is a grid of square, regarded as a perfect figure. It is conceived to be a fundamental form in architecture and all other shapes are derived from it. The Vastupurusha Mandala offers the formula to determine the functions of the building in relation to its orientation. The *Vasturatnakara* assigns specific functions to each direction. The South-east for example, is dedicated to fire and North-east to the element water. Invariably, the correspondence with the elements would determine the position of the rooms in the house. The space assigned to the region of fire, for instance, would be used for building a kitchen or reserved as a source for heat and warmth. The *mandala* also serves as a guide to locate the buildings on site and determining the position of the shrines in a temple complex.

The image of Vastupurusha, one with mandala is drawn in the likeness of man. His head lies in the North-east in the mandala of 64 squares, the legs in the south-west, right hand in the North-west, left hand in the South-east and other parts of the body fill the square. Forty-five gods or deities are constituent of the body of Vastupurusha; their number necessarily is the same in the mandala of either 64 or 81 or any other number. Only the extent allotted to each of the deity differs but not their relative position in the plan.. After the completion of the building, the Vastupurusha Mandala functions as an iconic construct – a device for adoration.

1.6 The Shape

Vastu says a site should always be square, which is a plot with all sides with same length and each corner at 90 degrees is an ideal one. It is very auspicious and brings health, wealth and happiness. It can be a rectangular with North-South length more than the East-West width, is also a good plot and auspicious too and will bring the happiness and prosperity. But a site should never be circular or of any irregular shape.

NW	N	NE
Air		Water
W	Space	E
	Brahmasthaan	
Earth		Fire
SW	S	SE

Vastu suggests that each direction has its own driving force or each element is represented by one direction.

Water	:	North-east
Fire	:	South-east
Earth	:	South-west
Air	:	North-west
Space	:	Brahmasthaan

1.7 The Open Space around the Building

We have to carefully examine the space given to us around the building and make sure that maximum space is left in North and East side and less on South and West sides. The construction should never be on the northern and eastern wall as this violates the basic principle of Vastu. The left area in North should not be less compared to the open area left in the South, as this is very bad according to Vastu so one must correct its defect before developing the plan.

1.8 The Proportion

The ratio between the length and breadth of the building should normally be 1:1 or 1:1.5 or maximum up to 1:2, it should never exceed this limit in any circumstance, otherwise it will become a 'long bar' shaped plot and is not at all auspicious for anyone. The building dimension should preferably be longer in North-South and shorter in East-West.

1.9 The Projections

The projections can be negative or positive depending on the direction in which the plot is projected. The projections should be taken care of, as wrong projections create the negative energy and thus will affect the life of the inmates.

- ❖ Plots with North-east corner projected towards North or East are very good. It always ensures health, wealth, name, fame and all round prosperity.
- ❖ Extension or projection to South-west is not good as it may cause loss of health, money and other unbearable problems. Projection of South-west corner towards South brings misery to the women folk in the house. Projection of South-west corner towards West brings name to males and mental problems to women and loss of wealth. Projection towards South and West creates problems like accidents and loss of wealth.

- Extension to South-east may cause fire, accidents, court litigation and thefts. Extension of South-east corner towards South affects the health adversely and makes their earning difficult.
- Projection to North-west is also bad as it may cause mental agony and heavy expense. Projection of North-west towards North are not good at all. Women will suffer from many problems – heavy expenditure and mental problems will increase. Extension of North-west towards West are good for women, women organisation and politicians.
- To summarise, only extension in North-east, North or East is auspicious and brings happiness and prosperity but care must be taken not to project North-east corner too far to affect the balance of the plot and rest of the other extension causing the ill-effects on the inmates.

1.10 The Retraction

Retraction is cutting of any of the corner of the plot. Just like the extension of plot affects the users of the building, retraction of different sides or corners has a great influence on the fortune of the inmates.

- A plot, which is chopped off in the North-east should never be purchased as that will always hinder the prospects and progress of the family and will create unhappiness all around, mental worry, children and wealth, both will be lost.
- A plot, which is cut off in the North-west corner will always bring the diseases, loss of wealth and the maximum fear of fire.
- A plot that is retracted in the South-east corner will bring poverty and disease.

- A plot that has North-west corner chopped off will always bring ill health of wife, mental worries and unhappiness.

1.11 The Basic Vastu Principles

- The North-east corner should never be truncated or made heavy.
- The heavy structures should be placed in the southern, western, South-west sides of the plot.
- The brahmasthaan (the central point) should always be left free or very light objects should be put there.
- The water in the East, North and North-east side is very good.
- The shape of the plot, its project and retraction are the major issues in choosing it.

1.12 The Doors

- The best thing is if the maximum number of doors and windows open in North and East sides of the building as compared to the South and the West side.
- The number of doors and windows in the house should be in even numbers like 2, 4, 6, 8, etc.
- While fixing the doorframes in an internal wall, it must be ensured that the doorframe is not fixed contiguous to the main wall of the house. At least a minimum of 4" pad should be built before fixing the doorframe to a lateral wall.
- Doors should not be placed in the centre of the wall; they should always be off centered.

Vastu Shastra ensures optimum utilisation of material resources in accordance with the shape of the building, the area to be utilised, the dimensions, symmetry of doors and windows and amalgamation with the structures both inside and outside. If the structure is so designed that the positive forces override the negative forces then there is a beneficial release of bio-energy, which helps all the inmates to be healthy. Vastu Shastra is of the belief that your home should be designed in a manner such that positive forces override negative forces, which leads to a positive cosmic field which infuses the residents with contentment and prosperity. The principles of Vastu when applied can guide you to create a positive atmosphere in your house.

2. THE ANCIENT AND SCIENTIFIC APPROACH TO VASTU SHASTRA

Vastu Shastra gives practical guidelines on site selection, orientation of the building, its contouring level, the conditions related to climatology and micro weather. Arrangements of rooms in relation to different activities performed there, the placement of furniture, colour scheme in residential properties. Position of machinery, boilers, furnaces, storage of raw materials, finished products, position of the staff, owner, administration in commercial places. Thus, it suggests the living conditions and standards in all the areas.

In Vastu Shastra, East and North directions are given great importance. The East is the gateway to the sun's rays and North is identified as pole star, the roof of the world.

2.1 The Ancient Approach

Our ancient sages believed that *Vastu Purusha* exists in each and every plot with his physical posture as head in North-east corner and folded legs in South-west portion. The whole body occupies the *Vastu Purusha Mandala* with abdomen lying in the centre. The *mandala* generally consists of 64, 81 *yogini* or squares and each square represents different application in relation with North orientation.

If we consider the nine directions, this is one of the principles that:

- The North-east portion should be left empty or very light and all the heavy and heaviest things should be placed in South-west corner, as this is the place of earth element.
- More space should be left in North and East portions than in South and West side.
- There is one another important principle that the slope of the building should be towards East, North-east, North.
- The master bedroom should be in the South-west corner and the puja room in North-east corner of the house.
- The bathroom should be in North-west direction.
- The kitchen should be in South-east direction.
- One should never sleep with the head in North direction.

These are only a few little principles that we follow in Vastu, I am just proving them scientifically. If I take the whole Vastu principles, I would have ended in writing an encyclopaedia (Refer to diagram under 1.5).

2.2 The Scientific Approach

Vastu comprises five natural elements – earth, water, fire, air and space. Each of the elements corresponds to a natural force that affects our lives. Our ascendants were great scientists and they understood the effect of the natural forces on the lives of human beings. They are:

Earth : Magnetic field of the earth
Water : Gravitational attraction of the earth
Fire : Solar radiation
Air : Wind energy
Space : Cosmic radiation

The other energies are:

Lunar energy

Electric energy

Magnetic energy
Thermal energy
Wind energy

The effect of the Vastu is permanent, because the earth has been revolving round the sun, in geo-stationary orbit for over 400 crores years creating the magnetic effect caused by the rotation.

2.3 The Magnetic Field

Earth is a magnet. It has a North Pole and a South Pole. The surface of the earth has magnetic grids called Hartman grids. According to trigonometry, the value of $\sin q = 1$ when $q = 90$ degrees, $\sin q = 0$ when $q = 0$ degrees, where q is the angle of deviation.

So the result is that any object which is in alignment with, the North-South pole of the earth, is said to have a maximum advantage over any other structure having a slightest deviation. This is because for any other deviation, $\sin q < 1$.

The magnetic lines of forces move from North to South, they are uniform at the centre and concentrated at the poles. Its always advisable that a man should sleep in North-South axis as man is a conductor and he moves in the magnetic field and as per Faraday's Laws of Electromagnetic Induction, a conductor moving in the magnetic field develops a current. But a person should not sleep with his head towards North, as head is our North Pole and similar poles repel each other, thus it will reverse the circulation of blood and disturb the sleep.

The master bedroom should be in South as the magnetic lines of forces are concentrated in the South Pole and thus the person occupying there will have the maximum benefit on the circulation of blood.

A square plot is considered to be the best as the magnetic lines of forces move from one side to another uniformly and evenly covering the major portion of the house. The irregular shapes should be avoided as the magnetic lines of forces get distracted.

The behaviour of an individual is conditioned by the electromagnetic frequencies generated at micro levels of the human brain. The North east is treated as the direction of goodness.

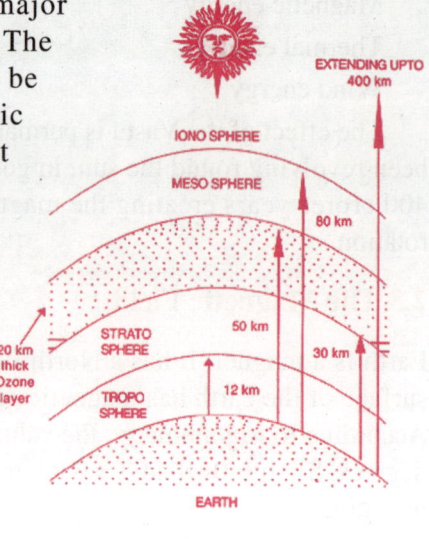

Now the studies show that the stress concentration of interacting energies is minimum in this direction and maximum in South-west. Low temperatures and stable geo-magnetic flux lines mark the North-east zone while the South-west direction represents a zone of maximum temperature and analogous magnetic field lines.

The instability increases as we move from the North-east to East to the South-east to South to the South-west to West to North and to the North-east. Vastu Shastra utilises this naturally happening gradations of energy balance and imbalance.

The East is the source of solar, ultraviolet rays, and the North is the source of magnetic energy. We benefit by keeping our environment open to this life supporting energies. The harmful infrared rays, which come from the South, and the destructive gamma rays, coming from the West, cause disruption within the environment and our bodies. Using the principles of Vastu Shastra, we protect ourselves from these rays.

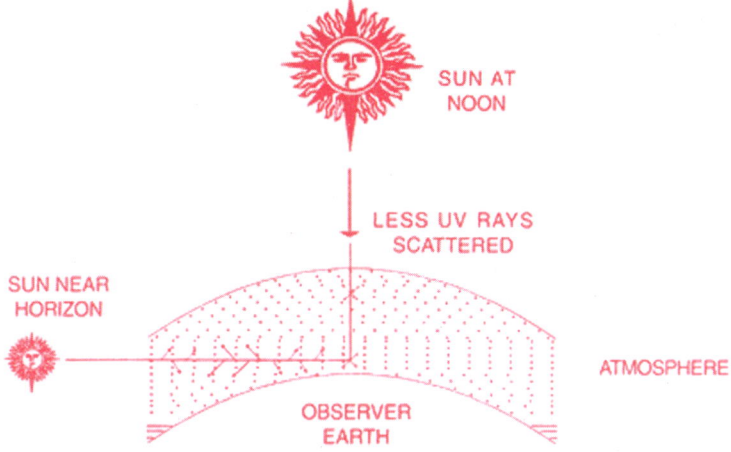

The slope should be towards East as the life sustaining electromagnetic vibrations from the early morning sun are available for only two and half hours immediately after sunrise and are likely to be interrupted by this reverse slope.

One should leave a lot of space in the East/North-east as the sun is the only source of vitamin D and infrared rays and if there is no obstacle in the said directions, mankind will be benefited with the natural sources.

2.4 Solar Radiation

Sun is the source of energy and its rays are called electromagnetic or radiations. These radiations constitute different characters like gamma rays, X-rays, ultraviolet rays, infrared rays, VIBGYOR, microwaves and radio waves.

The only visible part of this whole spectrum is VIBGYOR. It covers radiations from violet to red and is about 38 % of the total energy of the solar radiation. The rays beyond violet are called ultraviolet rays and rays beyond red are called infrared rays. Sun emits infrared rays till two hours of sunrise then these

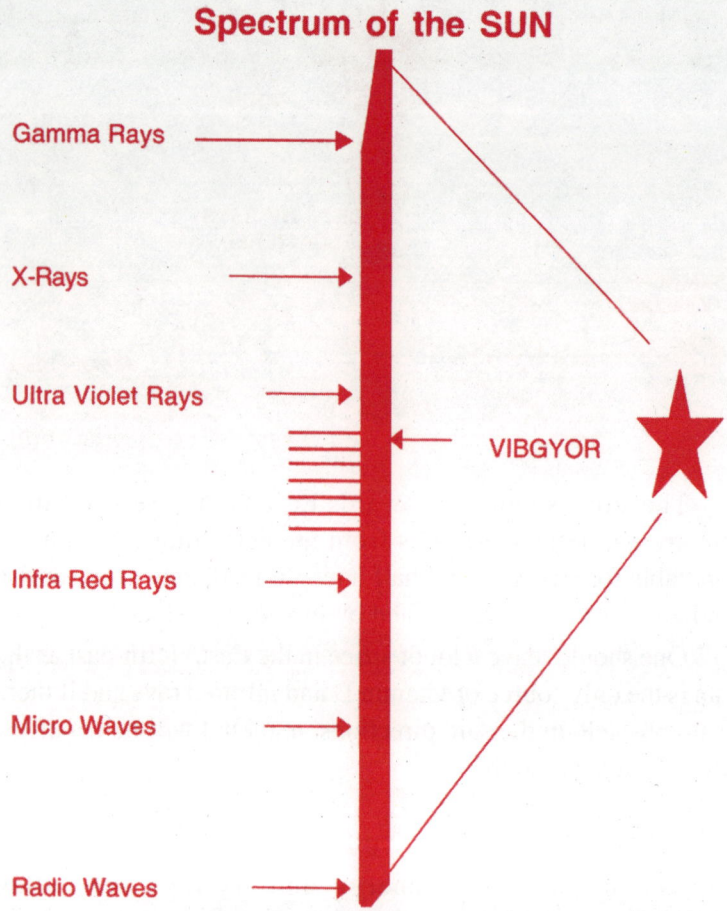

rays are converted into ultraviolet rays. Infrared rays are very useful for human beings and are the source of vitamin D. They activate and energise the body cells. Ultraviolet rays are harmful to human beings.

Infra-red rays are not allowed to pass through the atmosphere to a great extent. The carbon dioxide and the dust particles in the air absorb them. However some part of them reach the earth. Similarly ultraviolet rays are also absorbed by the ozone layer.

When our earth moves from one hemisphere to another, the distance between the sun and the earth is maximum in morning and evening and minimum in afternoon. The infrared rays therefore reach the earth in the morning from the East. So it is advisable to have maximum opening in the East precisely in North-east keeping in view the tilt of the earth on its axis.

So practically, it implies that our shelters should be designed in such a way that maximum of infrared rays are allowed to come in and ultraviolet rays are blocked. Water bodies should be kept in the North-east because the water absorbs the radiation and a body emits the same radiation as it absorbs. So the radiation that falls in water are multiplied and then are emitted back.

The slope should be in North/East for the same reason that, lower levels in these direction will have more water and thus more infrared rays will be absorbed.

It therefore becomes necessary to interpret the ancient wisdom in modern language so that people can understand, appreciate and can take advantage of it.

3 — A DEEP STUDY OF INTERNET

3.1 What is the Internet?

The Internet today is a continuous large-scale network of millions of computers that allows continuous communication across the globe. The Internet is the global "Network of Networks," linking thousands of computer networks together.

Currently, the Internet has more than 30 million users worldwide, and their number is growing rapidly. More than 100 countries are linked into exchanges of data, news and opinions on web servers. Unlike online services, which are centrally controlled, the Internet is decentralised by design. Each Internet computer, called a host, is independent. Its operators can choose which Internet services to provide to its local users and which local services to make available to the global Internet community. Remarkably, this anarchy by design works exceedingly well.

The WWW (World Wide Web) is the reason the Internet has become as popular as it is. The World Wide Web (WWW) is a part of the Internet, but is not the Internet itself. The Internet has many parts besides the WWW, such as e-mail, ftp, and Usenet. This is the part of the Internet that majority of users see — the websites and the pages that make them up. The web is the most widely used service of the Internet, which is accessed through a browser like *Internet Explorer* or *Netscape Navigator*. Today commercial industries, corporations, and residential users all communicate using the Internet.

The Internet is a super-network. It connects many smaller networks together and allows all the computers to exchange information with each other. To accomplish this all the computers on the Internet have to use a common set of rules for communication. Those rules are called protocols, and the Internet uses a set of protocols called TCP/IP (Transmission Control Protocol/Internet Protocol). Many people equate the World Wide Web with the Internet. In fact, the Internet is like the highway, and the World Wide Web is like a truck that uses that highway to get from place to place.

The web is an immense collection of web pages and thousands of new pages of information are added to the web every hour. Each page is placed on a *server*, a computer continually connected to the rest of the Web. The information is then available to anyone else with access to the Internet. Web pages can have a mixture of *text, graphics* and *multimedia*. Each Internet computer, called a host, is independent. Its operators can choose the Internet service from the services available to use and which local services to make available to the global Internet community. Nowadays, there's information available on practically anything you could be interested in somewhere on the web. You can use a search engine to find what you want.

3.2 How Internet Came into Being?

The Internet was the result of the imagination of the people in the early 1960s who saw great potential value in allowing computers to share information on research and development in scientific and military fields. The Internet was designed in part to provide a communications network that would be the most direct route available.

Computer experts, engineers, scientists, and librarians used the early Internet. There was nothing friendly about it. There were no home or office personal computers in those days, and anyone who used it, whether a computer professional or an engineer or scientist or librarian, had to learn to use a very complex system.

The foundations of the Internet were formed when *packet-switching networks* came into operation in the 1960s. Transmitted data is broken up into small packets of data, sent to its destination, and reassembled at the other side.

3.3 A Brief History of the Internet

> *A Generation, which ignores history, has no past and no future.*   *– Robert A. Heinlein*

The U.S. Department of Defence laid the foundation of the Internet roughly 30 years ago with a network called ARPANET. But the general public didn't use the Internet much until after the development of the World Wide Web in the early 1990s.

3.3.1 The Beginning: ARPANET

In 1957, the U.S. government formed the Advanced Research Projects Agency (ARPA), a segment of the Department of Defence charged with ensuring U.S. leadership in science and technology with military applications. In 1969, ARPA established ARPANET, the forerunner of the Internet.

3.3.2 Research and Education

ARPANET was a network that connected major computers at the University of California at Los Angeles, the University of California at Santa Barbara, Stanford Research Institute, and the University of Utah. Within a couple of years, several other educational and research institutions joined the network.

In response to the threat of nuclear attack, ARPANET was designed to allow continued communication if one or more sites were destroyed. Unlike today, when millions of people have access to the Internet from home, work, or their public library, ARPANET served only computer professionals, engineers, and scientists who knew their way around its complex workings.

3.3.3 Evolution

Throughout the 1970s, developers created the protocols used to transfer information over the Internet. By the early 1980s, Usenet newsgroups and electronic mail had been born. During the late 1980s, developers created indices, such as Archie and the Wide Area Information Server (WAIS), to keep track of the information on the Internet. To give users a friendly, easy-to-use interface to work with, the University of Minnesota created its Gopher, a simple menu system for accessing files, in 1991.

3.3.4 Tim Berners-Lee: Father of the Web

The World Wide Web came into being in 1991, thanks to the developer Tim Berners-Lee and others at the European Laboratory for Particle Physics, also known as Conseil Européenne pour la Recherche Nucléaire (CERN). The CERN team created the protocol based on hypertext that makes it possible to connect content on the Web with hyperlinks. Berners-Lee now directs the World Wide Web Consortium (W3C), a group of industry and university representatives that oversees the standards of Web technology.

Earlier, the Internet was limited to non-commercial uses because largely the National Science Foundation, the National Aeronautics and Space Administration, and the U.S. Department of Energy provided its backbone. But as independent networks began to spring up, users could access commercial websites without using the government-funded network. By the end of 1993, the first commercial online service provider, Delphi, offered full Internet access to its subscribers, and several other providers followed.

In June 1993, the Web boasted just 130 sites. By a year later, the number had risen to nearly 3,000. As of April 1998, there were more than 3.3 million sites on the Web.

3.3.5 Who has the Control on the Net?

No single authority controls the World Wide Web. Today's website authoring tools allow virtually anyone who has access to a computer and the Internet to post a website and contribute to the definition of what this medium is and what it can do. But the World Wide Web Consortium does oversee the development of Web technology.

With the development of tools that allow us to create websites without having any knowledge of hypertext mark-up language (HTML), this dream is being realised.

Keeping an eye on the standards of web technology is W3C, formed by Berners-Lee in 1994. An international group of industry and university representatives, W3C promotes the web by developing common protocols for transmitting information over the Internet. The consortium provides information, reference code, and prototype and sample applications to developers and users. It is hosted by the Massachusetts Institute of Technology's Laboratory for Computer Science in the United States, the Institute National de Recherche en Informatique et en Automatique in Europe, and the Keio University Shonan Fujisawa Campus in Japan.

In today's world of communication and multimedia, a company's reputation may lie in the realm of design. Businesses are growing on the web, and Internet is becoming a necessity these days. A website becomes a vital static for a company to bloom.

The buzz of high technology is everywhere. The Internet, in particular, is seen as a major catalyst of change in the way we live. It affects the way we run our business, communicate with each other, educate our children and interact with our government. The list is so long that it is almost futile to attempt to determine the general impact of the Internet on our society. In other words, by making even a small website, or visiting chat rooms, you can reach the world and can interact with millions of people of different professions.

Internet is one platform where the people of different countries having different culture following different paths of life meet without any conditions. The Internet's rate of growth has frequently been cited as "exponential." In August 1996, *Internet Info* reported that commercial domains in the United States had increased over 139 percent during the first half of the year alone.

3.4 Uses of Internet

The Internet is a powerful medium to reach the rapidly growing generation of computer-using Indians. "At the end of 2003, there are nearly 8 million web users in India, which is expected to rise to 40 million in 2005 and now India is the fourth largest internet user country. While the US continues to lead with nearly 200 million Internet users at the end of 2005, China and India are now in second and fourth place among Internet users", says eT Forecasts. This may seem small in comparison with the 1 billion total population, but it is more than the total population of many smaller countries, and it is increasing rapidly.

The Internet is best described as a network of computers which allow individuals to participate in a number of communication methods – sending and receiving e-mail, viewing and creating Web pages, having discussions through Usenet, using chat rooms for real time text conversations etc. Whether you conceive the Internet as a global communication tool or a cyberspace of international communities and cultures, this has n' number implications for international business and commerce, advertising, journalism, cross-cultural communication, education, democratic structures, entertainment, sociology, anthropology, the formation of virtual communities, self-expression and identity formation and development are among other examples. Considering that most of these users have only had Internet access for a few years or less, the growing importance of this technology over other domestic media is quite amazing.

The uses of the Internet are countless; it can do things beyond your imaginations. Broadly the websites are categorised into:
1. Communication
2. Business
3. Education
4. Information
5. Entertainment
6. Humanity Considerations
7. Sharing Data International

3.4.1 Communication

It was the major cause of the invention of the Internet. Internet has drawn the world so closer that the incident taking place in one part of the world can be viewed by you immediately and you can interact with that particular event by giving polls, your views, sharing a news with your near and dear ones in less than a minute. Can you think of anything faster than this service? The major paths of communication are:

A Deep Study of Internet 31

E-mail

Electronic mail works in much the same way as traditional mail does. Anyone is allowed to sign up for an e-mail address and then people can send you messages, or attach files from their computer and send them too. The main benefit of e-mail is the close to **instantaneous delivery** of messages that occurs. You can send e-mail to the other side of the world and it will arrive in less than a minute. You can also sign up to weekly newsletters and have information you want delivered right to your computer.

Internet telephony

This is useful for those whose family lives far away or the business is on the telephone conferencing. As Internet phones become more popular, long distance phone companies are losing money. The majority of Internet phones are offered free of charge, and long distance calls using your Internet phone only cost the amount you spend for your Internet connection fee, giving you the financial freedom.

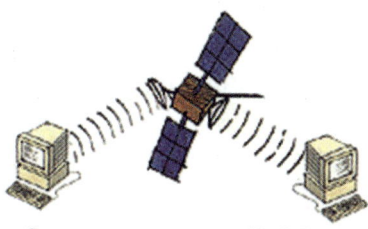

INTERNET AND E-MAIL

File Transfer Protocol

While web pages are transferred between computers using the http protocol, other types of files are sent using FTP. People can share files, like music and videos, among each other and the rest of the world by uploading them to a server and allowing others to download them to their own computers.

Internet Relay Chat

IRC is a service that allows you to connect to your chosen channel and talk in real-time to people with the same interests as you.

Usenet

USENET (UNIX User Network) is a system of bulletin boards where you and anyone else can post messages and people will read and reply to them. As with IRC, you will find boards set up for all sorts of groups of people.

Audio/Video Conferencing

Web Telephony is also used by businesses for audio conferencing. It allows employees from all over the world to engage in an audio conference simultaneously; therefore helping to speed up production while lowering overall business expenses.

Finding People

If you've lost track of any person, you can use one of the directory services to search the phone books of the entire United States. And now on many sites, phone book of many countries is there.

3.4.2 Business

Business is one field where the use of Internet has been very significant. Communication, research and information gathering, sourcing, and actual transaction execution are some of the broad areas in which companies have started to use the Internet in promoting their business. Successful businesses must also become on-line enterprises. Small businesses that use the Internet have grown 46% faster. Talk about anything and you will find it on Net. You can do online shopping, order anything from any part of the world.

What started as a small, in comparison to what the Internet is now, happening just a few short years ago has grown faster and bigger that anyone would want their child to grow. It has grown to the place where the child is almost unmanageable. In that growth, there are many businesses that have gone online without any idea of what their website is to do for them and how to use it to its best advantage.

E-commerce

This is the term given to the business done through Net. In today's current world, everything can be shopped through Internet, and everything is just a mouse click away. Electronic Commerce, whether B3B or B3C, is all about conducting financial transactions over the Web with suppliers and customers online. Compared to that, e-business carries a much broader meaning. It covers all the activities of an organisation that makes e-commerce possible.

EDI

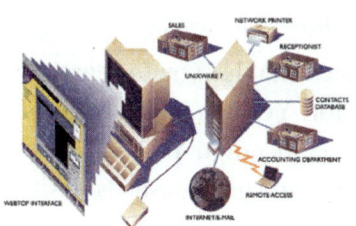

EDI (Electronic Data Interchange) allows the electronic transmission of orders, invoices and remittance information between businesses. The concept involves defining a standard format for the transmission of data between two businesses, which allows the whole transaction process to be automated.

B3B

It's clear that B3B E-commerce involves businesses selling things to each other over the Net, but there's a lot more to it than that. With so many businesses online, one of the problems is going to be of finding the best company to do business with. Simply scouring the Net looking for a company that exactly matches the criteria you are looking for is likely to be time-consuming and frustrating. What is needed is a sort of virtual middleman, or market maker that can bring together buyers and suppliers. And this is exactly what was developed. They perform the function of bringing buyers and sellers together, increasing market liquidity and generally reducing the cost of doing business online.

Service Providers

They are the organisations that provide people with different kind of services in different areas. For e.g. ISP, Internet Service Providers are the organisations that give access to the Internet by providing a part of their bandwidth to make use of the Net. Some of the ISP are VSNL, MTNL, Mantraonline, Satyam etc. and many more.

Service providers can be in any field. They allow you to make use of their resources. e.g., consultancy in any area like interior designing, Vastu consultancy.

Finding Companies/Business/Products/Services

New yellow page directory services enables you to search the type of company you are looking for. You can indicate the area code or zip code to help specify the location. You can simply type any service in any search engine and get thousands of sites.

Investment

People do financial researches, buy stock, and invest money. Some companies are online and trade their own shares. Investors are finding new ventures, and new ventures are finding capital.

3.4.3 Education

The Internet is a global computer network allowing communication with millions of computer users and access to resources from around the world. Use of the Internet can provide opportunities for inquiry-based learning. Students and teachers can network, study, and collaborate with others around the world.

Career Planning

Net is the source of the latest information. We have the information of anything new launched in the market and to move with the time, one has to be very uptodate in his knowledge. Through Internet you can have the information about the changing trends of the business, industry or any profession one wants to join. This is the fastest medium that keeps you updated with all the new trends of life.

Job Recruitment

In today's world unemployment is the major problem of our country. Either the company is not able to find good professionals or the unemployed people are not able to look for the job. These days employers and recruiters are making good use of the Internet and so should you. This article will help you learn how to use the Net as a job search tool. Many job hunters choose to put together an online resume. An online resume functions as a web page with hyperlinks that lead from one part of the resume to another, or to other locations on the Web.

Boon to the Researchers

The Internet is a wonderful resource for researchers of all kinds. From the information pool of Internet, one can look for anything. The Internet is an enormous library or collection of libraries through which one can access information.

Designing Websites

Providing Knowledge to Teachers

The Internet is a level playing field with an open libertarian ambience where "Information wants to be free." It provides more knowledge to the teachers with whom the career of a student and thus a future of a country lies. Thus the creators of the future of our country are also taking full use of Internet by enhancing their knowledge by reading the articles written by people all over the world, by communicating with other teachers, sharing ideas, gaining things and thus implementing them.

Guiding the Students

This is the best part of the Internet which is helping in planning a child's future. Students are gathering information, improving the ability to learn, understanding new and changing information technologies, evaluating the validity of information and are synthesising data acquired through the Internet into a meaningful whole.

The best example is Department of Education's National Institute on Post-secondary Education. The National Centre for Education Statistics has released a major survey on Distance Learning in Higher Education conducted by the U.S. Department of Education's National Institute on Post-secondary Education, Libraries, and Life-Long Learning.

In the 1970s EDC (Educational Development Centre) applied the educational techniques that had proven so effective in science, mathematics, and social studies to challenges in the areas of child development, gender equity, cross-cultural understanding, and health education.

The 1980's brought innovations in the areas of special education, workforce preparation, and numerous projects designed to prevent violence, substance abuse, and AIDS.

As EDC grows through the 1990's, projects continue to be build on the collaborative approach used in our earliest work.

Our programmes are not designed solely by theoreticians. They reflect the ideas of those who know the field as educators and learners.

Teaching through Net

It is a great resource for harnessing the teachable moments. Distance learning allows anyone with a computer and an Internet connection to learn new things from their home or work places whether to take a single course or to get a degree in the subject of their choice. One of the examples is the University of Leicester's New Distance Learning Program.

The various uses of Net in education can be categorised into:
- Student-centred education
- Project-based learning
- Integration of the curriculum
- Team teaching
- School based management
- Teaching social skills

3.4.4 Information

Internet is the pool of information whose depth can never be measured. One can get full information on any topic. The web is called the virtual library.

Directories

One of the easiest and safest methods of researching for relevant resources is by using directories that have already been vetted by other organisations. Directories are collections of resources organised into categories. Sometimes the directory will focus on one subject area. Others may collect and organise resources in a number of areas.

Creative Activities for Family

Parents can use the Internet as a natural tool to enhance communication with their children. You will find lot of things to talk about when you surf the Web together – mutual interests, current events, social and political issues, family concerns and values.

Medicinal Uses

Health care on the Internet has diversified and grown exponentially in the past two to three years. Physicians have been cautious about embracing the Internet. Recent AMA studies shows that the user numbers of the physicians have grown but 'skepticism' is still the word of choice to describe the attitude of the physicians to the role of the Internet in their practices. To the extent that physicians do use the Internet, the AMA study shows that they too use it as a source of information.

In the recent news heard, a doctor did an operation through the Net. Can one ever think of it? But yes, Internet has made it possible. A doctor in a country put the sensors on his body and operated a machine thousands of miles away near the patient. As the doctor proceeded his hands on the monitor showing the patient's part to be operated, so did the machine on the patient and the operation was successful!

Another life saving use of the Net is the use in emergency. If a person is not able to go to a doctor or if the doctor is not available in person, there are so many sites on the Net that provide you with urgent help. You type the problem and they will give you the first-aid help. What else can a person think beyond that!

Internet during Elections

This is an economical way to campaign rather than spending loads of money. During the 1996 election cycle, candidates for public office began to use the Internet as a campaign tool (Browning 1996; Casey 1996; Rash 1997). As the use of Internet grew among the general population, it was reasonable to expect that the 1998-election cycle would see increased use of this new medium by political candidates, and new methods and techniques developed to exploit its capabilities.

Travel Planner

One of the important uses of Net is to gather information about a place one would like to visit. One can have each and every information about any part of the world. And there are travel agents that will offer you good travelling packages.

Finding the Address

If you want to find an address of a particular person or individual, you can get it easily through the Net.

Walking Clubs

Walking clubs can use the Internet to find new members, communicate with club members, and to publicise their events. Walkers benefit from the club websites as they find out more about the organisation and opportunities. Clubs who have web sites report that they get a steady trickle of new members and new participants from the website, and get the most use out of e-mail between their club officers, members, and other walkers.

Providing Information for Getting Business

Another challenge for the people is to present the new information so that the distributors can use it easily at their customer locations. Most companies now a day's use Internet to provide information about their company and products.

Matrimonial Sites

Matrimony is the best example of merging of cultures. Internet provides that platform where people from all walks of life, meet, interact and sometimes get married. There are so many matrimonial sites where thousands of bachelors are waiting for the suitable matches and many of the marriages taking place are through these sites only.

3.4.5 Entertainment

This is one of the vast areas where the use of Internet is indispensable.

Games

It covers online games, sport sites especially the live coverage of any event. Cricket is the best example for Indians. Indians wherever situated in the world, which provides live updating of the score to know the current situation.

Music

Other entertainment sites like teenstation.com provides songs and videos.

Gamble

One of the major examples of entertainment is the lottery site. They are online lotto sites where a person can log on and can gamble. Others are the casino sites where you can play online casino.

Travel

Cities, towns, states, and countries are using the Web to put up (post) tourist and event information. Travellers find weather information, maps, transportation schedules and tickets, and museum hours online.

3.4.6 Humanity Consideration

Internet has a social use also. All the NGOs, (Non-government Organisation) communicate through Net. They have their own site through which they contact people and help them. One can contact them and provide them with charity through Net. Churches, synagogues, and other community organisations put up pages telling about themselves and inviting new people.

3.4.7 Sharing Data Internationally

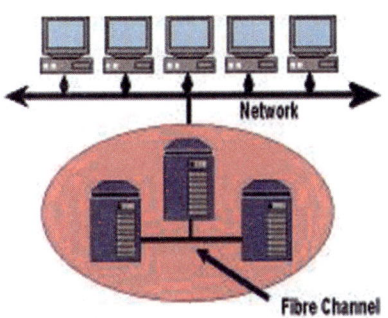

Necessity is the mother of Invention. Sharing data was the necessity, which invented the Internet. Sharing data can be a text, photo, clipping, audio, video and helps the people to communicate in a better way.

Sharing something through Net has overcome the problems like maintaining the paper work, faxing, posting, tensions of missing. Sharing can be inter-organisational like two organisations sharing some data; it can be intra-organisation like branches of a company in different places. Sharing can be personal. One can share the bio-data for a job or personal detail for a matrimony purpose!

Internet is such a vast topic that its uses cannot be confined to some pages. It has entered in our life slowly and is now the inseparable part of our lives. We do all our activities through Net and are connected globally.

3.4.8 Self-Defence – Military

This was the first reason for which the Internet was developed. Be it army, navy or the airforce, the Internet plays a major role in sharing the data from a remote place where no other access for information is there. There are certain sites created by the defence ministry which can be accessed only by the registered users and which contain the confidential messages used to transmit to the persons sitting on the borders.

A message reaches only in one minute through e-mail. Thus it is the fastest way to give messages. Now instead of talking on the phone, officers prefer to chat as this way they can discuss many things confidentially and for hours without being worried about the phone bills or overheard.

There are thousands of other uses also that we have left and these few are discussed only to show the importance of websites in today's life.

4 Extensive Study of the Websites

4.1 Designing A Website

A website is the image of a person's attitude, his perception and his business too. As a saying goes "tell me about your friends and I will tell you how you are", but nowadays people say "tell me about your website and we will tell about your business". A website should be such that it communicates necessary information effectively to the user, keeping in mind the ambient condition or the design of the site, which should be a very lively one.

Good sites happen when capable design meets memorable content. Before making a website, one should be very clear in his mind what the basic concept is. A strong website is one that clearly communicates your purpose to your customers and works in conjunction with your company's strategic plan.

Following points should be kept in mind before making a website.

4.1.1 What is a Website?

A group of web pages that collectively represent a company or an individual on the World Wide Web and that have been developed together to present information on specific subjects is also a website.

A website may include text, graphics, audio and video files, and hyperlinks to other web pages. Websites can range in size from as little as one page to a vast number of pages.

4.1.2 Set your Goals

What is the purpose of your site? Is your site an entertainment, education, e-commerce or an informative site? You should think about what you're trying to accomplish via Web and look for ways to reach that goal. Make sure the concept should accurately reflect your company's vision and image. The days of rushing onto the web are over, now this is the era of justification. With so many websites for choice, visitors are making judgement calls in a click of a mouse. If you cannot provide what they are looking for, or appear to have it, you will lose one.

4.1.3 Registering

One should plan to enter the web. If the business name is not registered, the name can effect the search engine rankings. One cannot make a presence on the Internet unless you have a name for your website (called a domain name), and a place for your information to reside so the world can access it. The place on the Internet that holds your information is called a host. The website host you choose provides one stop shopping for all your needs.

4.1.4 Domain Names

They are the web addresses of your site. They are the assigned IP address of your site and will be the name of the site. When picking out a domain name it is important to note how search engines give preference to these names and most list them alphabetically.

These are the prior things that are done before the commencement of the designing. Now designing is the most crucial part of a website and this is from where my research starts.

4.2 Initiating the Website

4.2.1 The Basic Outlining

Before initiating with the layout, one should have the basic concept in the mind on which the whole site is based. The concept should be such that it should be a "live site"; a person looking at it should make out the message it wants to convey without reading much of it.

4.2.2 The Organisation

The format of the site should be organised and easy to read and understandable. One should always use a table of contents or directory to the site. A website should always have a glossary that should explain all technical terms and acronyms. The pages should not be designed in such a way that it should be read by the latest browser software or by some specific program.

4.2.3 The Value of Site

It is impossible to define the 'value' as it is a synonym of 'quality' and no one can ever define a quality. Everyone has its own definition. A site liked by one person can get discarded by another, so measuring the 'value' of a web page is fundamentally impossible. But the satisfaction of the person who owns a site is the utmost.

4.2.4 The Source of Value

The information in the site should represent the basic value. That should be fully supported by navigation bar, all indexes should be well-maintained, search capability should be high, should have compatibility and well-structured content, then only one can take the benefit of the site.

4.2.5 The Colour and Graphics

The colours used in the website should be according to the business the website is into. The background should be kept simple and the contrast between the background and the text should be subtle. The graphics should be used in a synchronised manner, so that they flow with the design and it should not make the website difficult to read. Images should be described in the text and should have a connection with them.

4.2.6 The Speed.

A reader friendly design focuses on task-driven, upto the mark information, because timeliness is inevitably important to some of the surfers. The images or the video clips that are used in the design should be light and should not take much time to get download.

4.2.7 Getting the Re-visits

It's very hard to get visits again and again and is only possible if it is a user friendly site. Content rich, reader friendly websites are inherently high value websites because they strive to meet the information needs of their visitors in the perfect, most timely manner available. Such site always sees the repeated visitors and is likely to build a continuous traffic on the site by new visitors, which comes on the recommendations from the satisfied readers.

4.2.8 Uptodate Information

Nearly everyone wants the information. It is the single most common use of the web. But some people look something in very specific. Thus a site should reflect all the relevant information about the subject they are made for.

4.2.9 The Compatibility

As browser versions are multiplying, it is becoming more difficult to work according to all browsers. A website should be compatible with almost all the browsers. Thus the accessibility of the content will naturally propagate with simpler designs.

4.2.10 Easier to Use

Simpler tasks are always easy to master. The sustained growth of World Wide Web means that there is always a constant influx of the users. People who are using Net from years can handle any site but the new inexperienced users who are learning may face problems. A simple interface is always more inviting.

4.2.11 Easier to Download

It's more likely that a time-bounded user will simply abandon a slow-loading, elaborate site. New users are so impatient that they can't wait for long to download a site. Thus to make a site light, one should use light size pictures, graphics and light audio tracks.

If we take the site www.vastu-shastra.com; then this is a site, which is almost perfect in terms of naming a website, registering a domain, designing, value, colour and design, compatibility and speed.

If we consider the name, the name itself tells that it is Vastu Shastra site and it is registered with the same name. The designing, colour scheme and graphics are so perfect that it highlights the business the organisation is into and the site. The site gets downloaded very easily. This makes it a popular site with very good hits and queries.

5 INTRODUCTION TO WEB VASTU

In this book, efforts have been directed towards finding a common link between websites, Vastu science and astrology. This type of correlation serves its purpose in overcoming the unscientific fear. Faith and intellect are not two poles apart, but in fact are the two sides of the same mind. For the websites to bring business, the element in each quadrant must be honoured and they should be kept in balance as this creates powerful and beneficial conditions, which draws business towards the owner. On the other hand, an imbalance of the elements can create negative energies, which may have an adverse effect on the websites.

Why do users spend extra time on some websites than others and what makes them to come back to these sites again and again? Is it attractive graphics, eye-catching colours or the animation? While any of those things can be part of a good website, there are more elusive traits that can transform a good website into a great website and it can be done with the help of Vastu Shastra.

Vastu and Internet, both are very deep sciences and my research is to combine the modern with the Vedic culture to give a better perspective of the both.

5.1 The Five Elements

We all know that the five elements that comprise the human and the world are called the *paanchbhootas*. Similarly every website has its own *paanchbhootas* and a balance has to be maintained to achieve the desired results. Any disturbance in any of the element may result in negative consequences. Let us discuss them in detail.

5.1.1 Earth *(Bhumi)*

The earth is the mother of all, which has everything in herself. It is the basis of everything and it is from here, that anything gets started. Earth is the element of the mother and child relationship. Similarly here, I categorise the first element earth of the websites as the basic **LAYOUT** that contains the whole of the designing in itself, whether it be a front end or the back end. A layout is the physical placement or arrangement of graphics, fonts, code, colours. It is a drawing that indicates the relative positions of the element. The basic design of any website initiates from the layout. As without the earth, nothing is possible similarly without a layout, no website is not possible, it is the basic starting point of any designing.

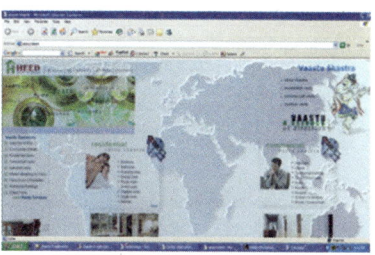

5.1.2 Water *(Jal)*

The water is the basis of every life on the earth, is the part of every living creature and forms ¾ part of the body's weight. Maximum portion of the earth is water. Similarly here, I categorise the second element *water* of the websites as the **TEXT** and the **GRAPHICS** without which no website is possible. It is the blood of every designing. The text is the

oxygen and the graphics haemoglobin of the blood that flows in a website. It is a very powerful element to use, it should always be clear and free flowing, never let it go stagnant, that is, there should be a rhythm of the graphics and the fonts and it should be placed in a synchronised manner.

5.1.3 Air *(Vaayu)*

The air is a very powerful life source and comprises lot of gases and sensitive elements, controls the temperature and humidity. As air represents movement and we cannot see the air but can feel the presence, a slight 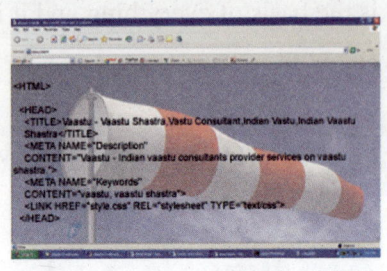 change in its constituent can change the properties. Similarly here, I categorise the third element air of the websites as the **BACKEND** or **HTML CONSTRUCTION**, without which one can never think of a site. We cannot see the HTML coding directly on the site but we can feel the presence and a slight change in any of the code in HTML that can change the look and the feel of the whole website.

5.1.4 Fire *(Sun)*

The fire is the strongest of all elements and represents liveliness or the life. It also represents the vision and the fame and circulates energy in the form of heat, light and colours. Similarly here, I categorise the fourth element 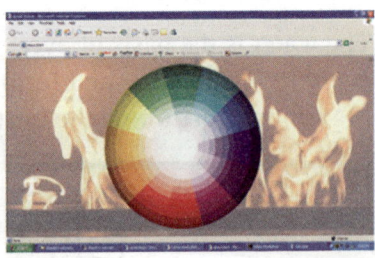 fire of the websites as the **COLOUR.** It represents the light, that is the sun. It provides the life to a design and is the strongest of all. Be it a poor layout but if colour combination is good, one

Introduction to Web Vastu   51

feels to look at it. As it is said that sun is a source of mental energy too, similarly colours also tell your mental level and have the power to even change your mood.

5.1.5 Space *(Aakash)*

The space is the creator of all the elements and provides shelter and comfort. It is the most widely spread over the five basic elements. Similarly here, I categorise the element space of the

websites as the **URL** or the **DOMAIN NAME**, that is the name of the site which comprises the other entire element. Like in the space, the solar system exists and so in the URL the business exists. The Internet is a huge galaxy in which the websites are small elements with different names. As a person is known by his name not by his individual body, similarly the URL address or its name categorises a website.

There is an invisible and constant relation between these elements within a website design. Thus, one can improve the business conditions by properly designing the websites by understanding the effectiveness of these five forces.

5.2 The Orientation

The orientation or the direction plays a major role in governing the layout according to Vastu. The orientation is establishing correct relationship in direction with reference to points of the compass. It is the awareness of one's environment and/or situation, along with the ability to use this information appropriately in a functional setting.

5.3 Why North

As already seen, there are eight directions that are shown in the figure and discussed earlier. They are the static directions which never changes. We always consider the North as the top of the page if you keep it in a readable position, this is the universal norm. If you keep any page on the map of the world, North is always the topside. Why to go far, in our body also. Our head always represents the North and our legs the South. Right hand is East and left one is West. That's why it is always said that one should never sleep with his head towards North as similar poles repel each other and the magnetic lines of forces interfere with the iron present in our body and thus disturb the blood circulation.

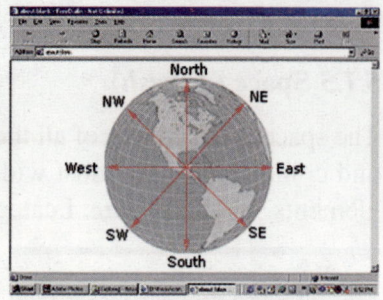

The major eight directions that one must always consider are the North, North-east, East, South-east, South, South-west, West, North-west.

Every direction has its own God who has its own governing planet and particular characteristics. People devote more time and attention on the minute details of foundation, structure, appearance of the building, going into detailed examination as to whether such a house or building which they are going to build will bring them prosperity, health, wealth, wisdom, happiness, peace or not. Similarly websites should be carefully designed and minutely checked so that they can perform their work efficiently for what they are been made for.

5.4 The Shape

The shape is the visual appearance of something. It is an area that is contained within an implied line or is seen and identified because of colour or value change. Shapes have two dimensions, length and width, and can be geometric or have a free form.

As Vastu suggests that the plot should either be rectangular or square to get the maximum benefit of the space, similarly a website should be either rectangular or square. The virtues of simplicity are well-known.

5.5 The Graphic Mandalas

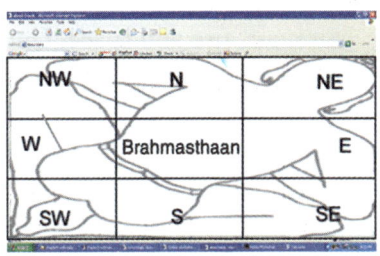

The Vastu Purusha Mandala is a grid of square, regarded as a perfect figure and offered the formula to determine the functions of the building in relation to its orientation. The Vasturatnakara assigns specific functions to each direction.

Similarly a website page is divided into a square grid which is been named as the **GRAPHIC MANDALAS**. Each square represents its own function. The basic division is of 9 parts and it keeps on dividing further, that is in a site at least 9 graphic *mandalas* are there. The graphic *mandala* can be defined as "a collection of squares, which attempt to facilitate the translation of graphical concepts into website form." This law of proportions and rhythmic ordering of elements now will change the concepts of designing.

7	8	1
6	9	2
5	4	3

For the websites to bring business element in each quadrant must be honoured and they should be kept in balance as this creates powerful and beneficial conditions, which draw business towards the owner.

On the other hand, an imbalance of the elements can create negative energies, which may have an adverse effect on the websites.

5.6 Analysis According to Webvastu

The world comprises five basic elements, also known as the *paanchbhootas*. They are earth, water, air, fire and space. Out of the nine planets, our planet has life because of the presence of these five elements. Similarly, I have tried to prove that every website has five elements and any disturbance in any of these established elements can cause an imbalance in the site that affects the website business directly.

I have tried to find out that how the orientations, planets, colours, name, date and time have an effect on the success of any website. Then analysis should be done keeping in mind the nature of the business and the planets governing that business.

The research done by me is been proved by the statistical data, which is mentioned with the name of the website in the beginning of every case site as *HITS* and *QUERIES*. Statistics or STATS is the mathematical term that tells about the performance in terms of visitors visiting that particular site. Hits is the average number of clicks on the site per day / per month and queries are the inquiry sent by the visitor through the site to the company regarding their products / services.

To begin with, first I have taken a particular site into a particular business governed by a specific planet. Then the site is divided into nine *mandalas* (9 parts), that is nine *graphic mandalas*. Each *mandala* has been studied very carefully and thoroughly.

The Five Elements of WEBVASTU

I have defined the five elements of the site as under:

- *EARTH* : Layout
- *WATER* : Fonts and Graphics
- *AIR* : HTML
- *FIRE* : Colours
- *SPACE* : Name

The *EARTH* element comprises all the nine directions and I have studied them all deeply according to Vastu and have formulated that the look and the feel of the website is very important if we consider the layout.

Like we say that according to Vastu the NE should be very light, similarly in a website the NE should be empty or should be occupied with the photographs which gives a very light and soft feeling. Though the size of the image also matters which defines the weight of the graphic which is measured in the unit called BYTES and 1000 bytes = 1 KB or KILOBYTE.

In the *WATER* element, I have studied the font shape and size and the feel of the graphics placed in a website. Photographs are the characters of the mind and in a website they become graphics and form character of the design. As stagnant water is boring and running water is full of life, so are the graphics. There should be a rhythm, a concept in the placement of the graphics.

In the *AIR* element, the HTML coding is the backend of any site, i.e., the site is constructed through this programming. The HTML described here is only the tip of the iceberg meaning it is just a part of the whole programming. The coding described here only explains that how any flaw in the website can be corrected by the change in the programming language. If you want to see the HTML coding, go to any browser, on the top menu, there is VIEW menu and inside that is a command called 'source'. Click right on the browser and there is a direct option of 'view source' which shows about the HTML programming.

In the *FIRE* element, I have tried to prove that how colours play a very important part in the business of the websites. There is a governing planet of every business and every planet is represented by a particular colour. So it is necessary that the colour you choose for your website should be favourable to the governing planet of the business and to the planet of the website. The colour scheme should be chosen very carefully.

In the *SPACE* element, the name plays a very critical role. The name of the website should be favourable to the name of the owner, that is, the governing planet of the zodiac of the name of the website should be a friend of the governing planet of the zodiac of the name of the owner.

The *TIME* is another factor that plays a very essential role in designing and hosting a site. As in Vastu, when a house is constructed, there is a particular auspicious time for putting the foundation stone and for entering the new house. Likely time should be considered before the commencement of the design and hosting.

Broadly the month is divided into two phases – *Shukla Paksh* and the *Krishna Paksha*. The Shukla Paksh is from the new moon to full moon that is when the moon is in ascending position. And the Krishna Paksha is the time when moon moves from full moon phase to no moon, that is the descending movement of the moon. In our Vedas, it is described that Shukla Paksh is auspicious for starting any thing new and Krishna Paksh should be avoided.

Introduction to Web Vastu 57

An example is given below.

This is a site www.sereneinteriors.com and the analysis of this site is given below.

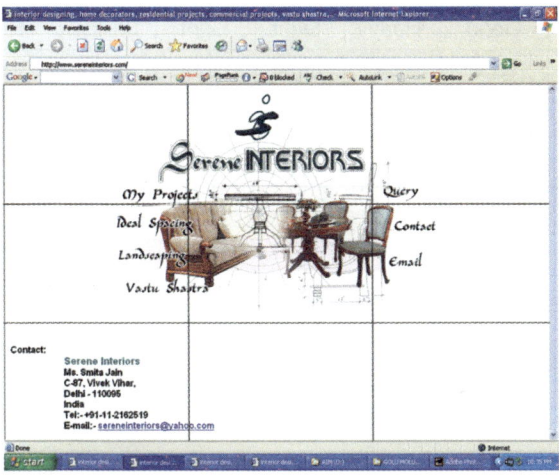

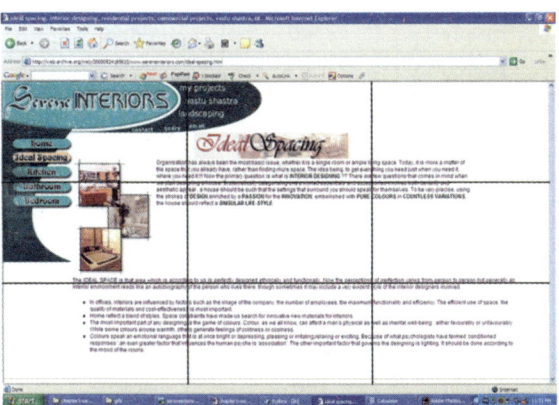

SITE URL	www.sereneinteriors.com
NATURE OF BUSINESS	Interior/furniture designing and manufacturing
CONTACT PERSON	Ms. Smita Jain

EARTH

Layout

Page	Layout	North	East	South	West	Bhrmasthan
Home	Good	Heavy	Light	Light	Partial	Heaviest
Inner	Nice	Ok	Light	Light	Heavy	Light

North

Page	Look	Bytes	Colour	Points(10)
Home	Heavy	12 Kb	White, Green	3
Inner	Ok	Text	Green	6

North-east

Page	Look	Bytes	Colour	Points(10)
Home	Empty	1 Kb	White	9
Inner	Empty	1 Kb	White	9

East

Page	Look	Bytes	Colour	Points(10)
Home	Empty	1kb	White	8
Inner	Empty	1 Kb	White	8

South-east

Page	Look	Bytes	Colour	Points(10)
Home	Empty	1 Kb	White	3
Inner	Empty	1 Kb	White	3

South

Page	Look	Bytes	Colour	Points(10)
Home	Empty	1 Kb	White	1
Inner	Empty	1 Kb	White	1

South-west

Page	Look	Bytes	Colour	Points(10)
Home	Light	Text	White	1
Inner	Empty	Text	White	1

West

Page	Look	Bytes	Colour	Points(10)
Home	Light	4 Kb	Light	1
Inner	Heavy	12 Kb	Green	7

North-west

Page	Look	Bytes	Colour	Points(10)
Home	Empty	1 Kb	White	2
Inner	Heavy	12 Kb	White	6

Bhrmasthaan

Page	Look	Bytes	Colour	Points(10)
Home	Heaviest	12 Kb	White	0
Inner	Light	Text	White	9

WATER

Text and Graphics

- Text is ok and has no problems with typography.
- Graphics are not properly balanced, that's why the site is not getting enough queries.

AIR

HTML Construction

The problem in this site is that the Brahmasthaan is the heaviest, so by just changing an attribute, the collage shifts to left, thus making the Brahmasthaan light and West heavy.

<!DOCTYPE HTML PUBLIC "-//SoftQuad//DTD HoTMetaL PRO 4.0::19970714::extensions to HTML 4.0// EN"

"hmpro4.dtd">
<HTML>
<HEAD>
<BASE HREF="http://www.sereneinteriors.com/">

<TITLE>interior designing, home decorators, residential projects, commercial projects, Vastu Shastra, landscaping, furniture designing, layouts, ideal spacing - Serene Interiors</TITLE>

<META NAME="Keywords" CONTENT="interior designer, residential projects, official projects, commerical projects, showrooms, offices, house interior, furniture designing, interior desigining, layouts, Vastu Shastra, home decorators, ideal kitchen, ideal spacing, landscaping, serene interiors, indiamart">

<META NAME="Description" CONTENT="Serene Interiors - Indian interior designers providing designs for bedrooms, bathrooms, kitchen, furniture designing, interior decor, houses, residential projects, official projects, commerical projects, showrooms, offices">

<META NAME="Author" CONTENT="Raj Kumar Narang, www.indiamart.com">

</HEAD>
<BODY BGCOLOR="#FFFFFF">
<DIV ALIGN="CENTER"><IMG SRC="gifs/serene-logo-lft-space.gif" ALT="serene interiors, furniture designing, interior desiging, layouts" BORDER="0" HSPACE="0" VSPACE="0" WIDTH="181" HEIGHT ="81"> <IMG SRC="gifs/serene-logo.gif" ALT="Serene Interiors Logo - The interior designers" BORDER="0" HSPACE="0" VSPACE="0" WIDTH="155" HEIGHT= "81"> <IMG SRC="gifs/zero2.gif" BORDER="0" HEIGHT="1" WIDTH="263">

<IMG SRC="gifs/serene-interiors-txt.gif" ALT="Serene Interiors - interior designing, furniture designing, interior decorators, designing layouts" VSPACE="0" HSPACE="0" BORDER="0" WIDTH="600" HEIGHT="81">

Introduction to Web Vastu 61

<A HREF=" my-projects.html" TARGET=""" ONMOUSEOVER ="itson('img1','onimage1');itson ('imga','onimagea');" ONMOUSEOUT="itson('img1',' offimage1');itson('imga','offimagea');"> <IMG SRC="gifs/ myprojects-txt.gif" ALT="My Projects" BORDER="0" HSPACE="0" VSPACE="0" NAME="img1" WIDTH=" 181" HEIGHT="46"></A><IMG SRC="gifs/myproject-query.gif" ALT="residential projects, commercial projects, vastu shastra, landscaping, room decorators" VSPACE="0" HSPACE="0" BORDER="0" WIDTH="317" HEIGHT= "46"><A HREF=" query.html" TARGET=""" ONMOUSEOVER =" itson ('img2','onimage2');itson ('imga','onimageb');" ONMOUSEOUT="itson('img2','offimage2');itson ('imga',' offimageb');"><IMG SRC="gifs/query-txt.gif" ALT="Query" BORDER="0" HSPACE="0" VSPACE="0" NAME="img2" WIDTH="102" HEIGHT="46"></A>
<A HREF="ideal-spacing.html" TARGET=""" ONMOUSEOUT ="itson('img3','offimage3');itson('imga',' offimagec');" ONMOUSEOVER=" itson('img3','onimage3'); itson('imga', 'onimagec');"> <IMG SRC="gifs/ideal-spacing. gif" ALT="Ideal Spacing" VSPACE="0" HSPACE="0" BORDER="0" NAME="img3" WIDTH="181" HEIGHT ="50"></A><IMG SRC="gifs/contact-ideal-spacing.gif" ALT="room decoration, living room, kitchen, bathroom, bedroom, interior decorator" BORDER="0" HSPACE="0" VSPACE="0" NAME="imga" WIDTH="317" HEIGHT ="50"><A HREF="#contact" TARGET=""" ONMOUSEOUT ="itson('img4','offimage4');itson ('imga','offimaged');" ONMOUSEOVER="itson('img4','onimage4');itson ('imga','onimaged');"><IMG SRC="gifs/contact-txt.gif" ALT="Contact" VSPACE="0" HSPACE="0" BORDER="0" NAME="img4" WIDTH="102" HEIGHT="50"></A>
<A HREF="landscaping.html" TARGET=""" ONMOUSEOVER="itson('img5','onimage5');itson('imga',' onimagee');" ONMOUSEOUT="itson('img5','offimage5');

itson('imga','offimagee');"><IMG SRC="gifs/landscaping-txt.gif" ALT="Landscaping" BORDER="0" HSPACE="0" VSPACE="0" NAME="img5" WIDTH="181" HEIGHT="58"></A><IMG SRC="gifs/landscaping-email.gif" ALT=" interior decorations, flooring of rooms, home furnishing, home decorating" VSPACE="0" HSPACE="0" BORDER="0" WIDTH="317" HEIGHT="58"><A HREF=" mailto:sereneinteriors@yahoo.com?subject=Query regarding Interior Desiging" TARGET="" ONMOUSEOVER="itson ('img6', 'onimage6'); itson('imga','onimagef');" ONMOUSEOUT=" itson('img6','offimage6');itson('imga', 'offimagef');"> <IMG SRC="gifs/email-txt.gif" ALT="Email" BORDER="0" HSPACE="0" VSPACE="0" NAME="img6" WIDTH="102" HEIGHT="58"></A>
   <A HREF="vastu-shastra.html" TARGET="" ONMOUSEOUT="itson('img7','offimage7');itson ('imga','offimageg');" ONMOUSEOVER=" itson('img7', 'onimage7');itson ('imga','onimageg');"><IMG SRC="gifs/vastu-shastra-txt.gif" ALT="Vastu Shastra" VSPACE="0" HSPACE="0" BORDER="0" NAME="img7" WIDTH="181" HEIGHT="73"></A><IMG SRC="gifs/vastu-shastra-rhtspace.gif" ALT="interior designers, designing layouts, landscaping, vastu shastra" BORDER="0" HSPACE="0" VSPACE="0" WIDTH="419" HEIGHT="73">

   <A NAME="contact"></A>
   <DIV ALIGN="JUSTIFY"><STRONG><FONT FACE="arial">Contact:
   </FONT></STRONG>
   <DIV ALIGN="CENTER">
   <TABLE WIDTH="80%" BORDER="0" VSPACE="0" HSPACE="0" CELLSPACING="0" CELLPADDING ="0">

```
<TR>
<TD><STRONG><FONT FACE="arial"><FONT SIZE="+1" FACE="aril" COLOR="#408080">Serene Interiors</FONT><BR>
Ms. Smita Jain<BR>
C-87, Vivek Vihar,<BR>
Delhi - 110095<BR>
India<BR>
Tel:- +91-11-2162519<BR>
E-mail:-
<A HREF="mailto:sereneinteriors@yahoo.com?subject = Query regarding Interior Desiging" TARGET="">sereneinteriors@yahoo.com</A></FONT></STRONG></TD>
</TR>
</TABLE></DIV></DIV></DIV>
</BODY>
<!— SOME SCRIPT SRC'S ON THIS PAGE HAVE BEEN REWRITTEN BY THE WAYBACK MACHINE
    OF THE INTERNET ARCHIVE IN ORDER TO PRESERVE THE TEMPORAL INTEGRITY OF THE SESSION. —>
<SCRIPT language="Javascript">
<!—
// FILE ARCHIVED ON 20000304120802 AND RETRIEVED FROM THE
// INTERNET ARCHIVE ON 20050929111659.
// JAVASCRIPT APPENDED BY WAYBACK MACHINE, COPYRIGHT INTERNET ARCHIVE.
// ALL OTHER CONTENT MAY ALSO BE PROTECTED BY COPYRIGHT (17 U.S.C.
// SECTION 108(a)(3)).
```

```
var sWayBackCGI = "http://web.archive.org/web/
20000304120802/";
function xLateUrl(aCollection, sProp) {
var i = 0;
for(i = 0; i < aCollection.length; i++)
if (aCollection[i][sProp].indexOf("mailto:") == -1 andand
aCollection[i][sProp].indexOf("javascript:") == -1)
aCollection[i][sProp] = sWayBackCGI + aCollection[i]
[sProp];}
if (document.links) xLateUrl(document.links, "href");
if (document.images) xLateUrl(document.images, "src");
if (document.embeds) xLateUrl(document.embeds, "src");
if (document.body andand document.body.background)
document.body.background = sWayBackCGI + document.
body.background;
//—>
</SCRIPT>
</HTML>
```

FIRE

Colours

Site Raashi/ Planet	Colour Used	Governing Planet of Business	Colour of Governing Planet	Relation	Colour Suggested
Aquqrius-Saturn	White, Green	Venus	Black	Friends	White, black, blue

SPACE

Name

Site Raashi/ Planet	Owner Name	Owner Raashi/ Planet	Relation
Aquarius-Saturn	Smita	Aquarius -Saturn	Neutral

TIME FACTOR

This site is hosted in Krishna Paksh.

Conclusions

- ❖ The site is not doing a good business and statistics are confirming it.
- ❖ The home page design is concentrated in the centre.
- ❖ In the home page, the North and Brahmasthaan are the heaviest.
- ❖ The South, South-west, West is all empty.
- ❖ In the inner pages, the South-west and South is all empty.

And the data proves that the site is not doing good business as it is getting only *2319 hits* and *11 queries* in one month, which is less than average.

This is a humble attempt in giving a glimpse of the fusion science, which I have named as **WEB VASTU**. I am only trying to smoothen people's business by making it more harmonious and thereby having gradual increase through websites. Destiny always prevails, but by implementing the Vastu concepts, one can enhance the business provided by websites. Therefore, it is advisable to follow Vastu to open the gates to a happy and prosperous life.

6 RESEARCH ON THE PROPOSED LAYOUT: THE EARTY ELEMENT

6.1 What is a Layout

A layout is the congenial setting of images, colour schemes, logos, tradenames and animations. It is the design or pattern of the placements of different elements. Web graphics must serve a function and should not be overloaded.

6.2 The Layout

The layout contains the different parts like graphics, fonts, colours, navigation buttons, logos and many more things and they should be placed in such a manner so that a rhythm flows in a site and it should not look congested. The following types are been described:

6.2.1 Navigation Buttons

They are the buttons or the images that can be clicked and are used to go to another page or graphic. They help the visitors to navigate the website. They should be designed in such a way that they are clearly visible and readable.

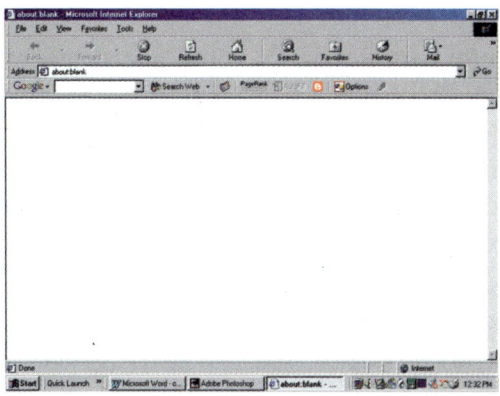

6.2.2 Logos

A logo is the symbol of a company and should be placed in such a way that it should neither get dominated by other graphics, nor dominate the other web graphics.

6.2.3 Graphics

A graphic, makes the webpage is inviting and visitor's eyes are automatically drawn on the photo. A site should have the balance of the graphics and should not be overloaded with them. Graphic images on your web page should serve a function that is directly related to your business.

6.2.4 Text

The text should be shown in such a way that a site should not become boring and the font size and style should be chosen carefully. The text in all your webpages should use the same typeface and same special effects if given.

The general rule is to keep the web page size between 40-60K. If you are a graphic designer, photographer, architect, or programmer, a 75K web page will still give a relatively fast download time on a 28.8 Kbps modem.

6.3 Layout according to Vastu

A good start for page design is to draw a rectangle of the same aspect ratio as a computer screen, or at least the usable part of it for your web page. The layout should be simple because simple is easier to use and handle, it is more stable, more compatible and less prone to errors. There are some of the sixes of the screen in pixels that are commonly used and they are converted into inches:

640 × 480 pixels	8.889 × 6.667 inches
800 × 600 pixels	11.11 × 8.33 inches
1024 × 768 pixels	14.22 × 10.66 inches
1280 × 768 pixels	17.77 × 10.77 inches
1280 × 1024 pixels	17.77 × 14.22 inches

The ratio between the length and breadth of the building should normally be 1:1 or 1:1.5 or maximum up to 1:2. It should not be more than this ratio otherwise the page is not considered balanced.

The major rules while designing a layout are following:

❖ The ratio of the width to height should not be more than 1:2.

❖ The North / North-east / East should be kept empty or filled with text or navigation buttons. Very light graphics can be placed here.

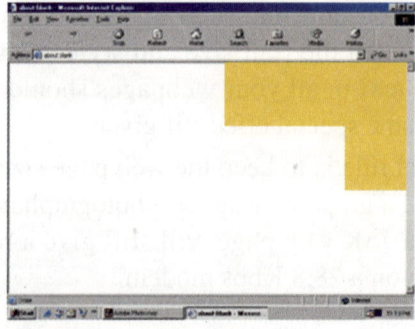

Research on the Proposed Layout: The Earth Element 69

The South / South-west / West should be made as heavy as possible.

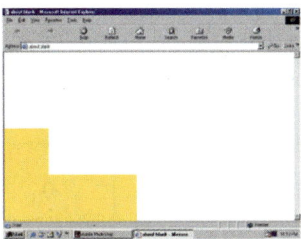

- ❖ The address should come in South/ South-west/ West and avoid more text.
- ❖ The brahmasthaan should not be occupied with heavy graphics or collage or any kind of image.

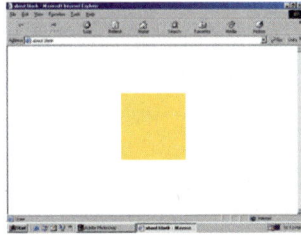

- ❖ There should not be any type of projection or retraction in the layout.
- ❖ Thus the base of the layout should be heavy than the top and it should be the heaviest.

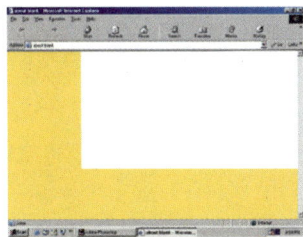

Designing Websites

The load in a layout should be distributed in a ratio, like North/East should get 25% of the whole layout, North-east should not have any weight, North-west can support 50 % of the load, South/West should be given 75% and the South-west should be the heaviest.

NW 50%	N 25%	NE -0
W 75%	+0	25% E
100% SW	75% S	50% SE

The rest of the things are discussed in other chapters in detail.

7. RESEARCH ON THE PROPOSED FONT/GRAPHICS: THE WATER ELEMENT

7.1 What are Fonts?

A font is the shape of characters which combine to form a word. They are also called the type and study of type is called the typography. Type is very important as it creates the feel of the web page. It attracts attention, sets the style and tone of a document. Netscape2 introduced the revolutionary FONT tag in 1995.

7.2 What are Graphics?

Any picture or image file within a Web page is called graphic.

In computing, the presentation of information which is not in character form. A graphic is a file containing a picture or photograph or picture or non-text item within a document. Most Web pages will contain a number of graphics. Type/ Graphic are very important part of a website as they can reinforce your image as a company or an individual as they tell everything about a design.

Arial
BAJORAN
Byfield
Comic Sans MS
Complex
Courier New
Futura XBLK BT
Gothic
Helvetica
Impact
Italic
Romantic
Vineta BT

7.2.1 It is Important

The right typeface/graphic develops interest in the people to read your message and view your website. The wrong typeface or bad typography can make even a very informative message to go unread.

7.2.2 It is the Image

A typeface/ graphic is the image of a company or an individual. It tells the type of profession the site is into. Like a serious dealing site will have straight measured words with very corporate photos and if it is a fun site, one will find very cursive characters with cartoon pictures.

7.2.3 It is the Personality

It shows the perception of the person. Changing a typeface/ graphic can make a site from casual to formal, serious to funny, conservative to modern. If a person uses a type/ graphic patterns consistently, people will start to associate that person with that particular typeface.

7.2.4 It is the Power

It has the strength of conveying and strengthening the message. It attracts attention, and helps in improving the image.

7.2.5 It is the Communication

Communication means telling the information and emotions about anything to others. A font/graphic is the best way to relay your message with particular feelings.

7.3 Types of Typeface

Good typography is just as important on a web page as it is in any other medium. The fact that it appears on a computer screen or on a piece of paper is immaterial, it should still be pleasing to look at and easy to read. In every situation where type is used in publishing, packaging, television etc., the designer has to take special care of the fonts.

From thousands of fonts available in the area, it is upto the designer to choose the relevant typeface that can easily communicate the business of the site in the first look.

7.3.1 Types of Graphics

The graphics cannot be categorised into groups, as there are endless and limitless photographs. They can be said as serious photos, funny photos, individual photo, environment photo and commercial pictures.

7.4 How to Choose the Typeface/Graphics

The words should make a good first and lasting impression. It is the thing that go into making you look good on the web. First of all the text should be precise and should have the clear content, correct grammar, spelling, and punctuation. Similarly with graphics, they should be to the point and should convey the message without reading the text.

7.4.1 The Purpose

The typeface/ graphic used by the designer should always solve the purpose of the design. It should communicate the feeling of the site in the first impression.

7.4.2 The Mood

One must know the impression one wants to make with the words and pictures. What moods do one wants to communicate? What feeling does one wants the readers to have while seeing and reading the website.

7.4.3 The Eligibility

A typeface should be chosen on these criteria. The words should be easy to read and provide a suitable background. Type should not overpower the text. Type can be beautiful and decorative but if it is difficult to read the text then it becomes distracting. It is absolutely the most important thing about the document that it should be easily read by anyone of any age with any kind of eyesight under any kind of lighting conditions. The typeface you choose must fit those criteria.

7.4.4 Easy to Download

The graphics should be placed in such a manner that they should not get clustered and the picture size should be light so that it can download easily and communicate better.

7.5 The Typography

The typography is not merely the study of the fonts but is the science of the letters, how they form to make a word and how words translate a sentence, sentence makes a paragraph and paragraph makes a page. For understanding this, we will have to know about some terms.

7.5.1 Aperture

Open space in a letter is called the counter or the aperture. This positive/negative space dictates how the letter is interpreted. Aperture relationship to character weight is fundamental in determining the quality of typeface.

7.5.2 Kerning

It is width in between the letters. A word should be ideally distanced, that is neither too close nor too far. For e.g. **Courier**, where all the characters are assigned the same width.

7.5.3 Tracking

It is letter spacing, that is equal throughout the entire word. Increasing the kerning can slow the reader down, can make the word fall apart.

7.5.4 Leading

It is the vertical space between lines of text. Amount of leading is informed by the line length.

7.5.5 Indentation

It is the white space that is given before starting a paragraph. Indentation carries a lot of meaning, especially in mail messages. Indents help keep your thoughts together.

7.5.6 Justified Text

The verb 'to justify' means aligning both margins. Justified text is both flush right and flush left.

7.6 The Guidelines for Designing Fonts

Sometimes a typeface works so well, it inspires designers of type to create a full range of related versions.

7.6.1 Typeface Family

A designer should use one typeface in a design to maintain the consistency. There are many typeface families, which comprise many styles, e.g. Jim Lyles at Bitstream has designed one such family, Prima. The Prima family includes twelve typefaces. A typeface family like Prima can enhance your web pages. There are Prima Sans for headlines, Prima Serif for text, and Prima Mono for contrast — HTML code, captions, whatever one wants.

7.6.2 Condensed and Extended Typefaces

When the words are more than the available space one can get more words on the page by using a condensed typeface.

When the space available is more than the words to be put in or you want your words to cover more of the page, or want to make a visual point, extended style is brought into consideration.

7.6.3 Bold and Italics

They are the tools to emphasise something on the web. One can make the headline bold or can make a word in Italics to highlight it. But underlining a word in a design is not a good sign as one can get confused with hyperlinks.

7.6.4 The Lesser the Better

Always try to use the less and appropriate text. The information should be broken up with headers and links. The lines of the text should be shorter and wide. The design of the layout should be such that the text does not appear in a single long block.

7.6.5 Set the Left Margin

A decent left margin should be left before the commencement. It makes it easier for your eye to 'catch' the left edge of the text as your eye moves down the page.

7.6.6 Specify Multiple Fonts

The users can have any of the machine e.g., Macintosh, Windows. The fonts designated should be commonly found on both the platforms. The font specified should be the one that looks ideal for the design and the most legible.

7.6.7 Relative Sizing

The flow of the text on a page varies from one machine to another and from one browser to another. This sometimes makes relative sizing a better choice than absolute sizing. Relative sizing adjusts the font size relative to the normal screen display.

7.7 The Basic Outlines

The use of appropriate fonts can enhance the design of the Web page. When selecting a font for the site, remember that text can help to convey a feeling or set a mood. There are some basic

guidelines which should be kept in mind before initiation of the selection of the font.
- ❖ Use the typeface, which is easier to read by everyone and interacts with the user.
- ❖ Use shorter blocks of text, as it is easy to read.
- ❖ Limit the number of fonts on the site to give it a professional look.
- ❖ The text should be between 10 and 12 point, with 11 point best for printing.
- ❖ Use enough leading and kerning to give it a synchronised feel.
- ❖ The lines should have the optimum characters between 30-70.

7.8 Fonts As Per Vastu

God has created the nature in a geometric pattern. All the things created by human gives message in one way or the other in Vastu language. Energy changes with the rhythm of the pattern, form, and shape, dimension, size, length, width, height of different characters and this is how the effect of Vastu comes in the typography.

It is important to understand the construction of the letters. Different parts of letters have identification purposes. They tell about the culture, trend, age, and personal preference.

The typeface used should be a proportionate font and all the characters should form some rhythm so that the person reading can flow with that rhythm.

7.8.1 The Size of the Fonts

The size of the fonts is a very important factor as the auspicious sizes have been defined as follows:

1:1	1:1.25
1:1.5	1:2

WEBVASTU

Keeping in view the balanced look, which is well-appreciated by a new watcher for the first time, it is suggested that the ratio between the width and the height of a letter should not exceed 1:1.5. This is an important tenant of Vastu that anything, which is against aesthetics or functional utility, cannot be Vastu friendly.

7.8.2 The Tilted Fonts

Right-tilted Fonts

The fonts are either straight or tilted in left or right. The straight things are always better, the right tilt is better as it represents the clockwise movement. A clockwise movement represents conservation of energy.

WEBVASTU

Left-tilted Fonts

The left tilt represents the anti clockwise movement thus frittering away of energy. With a view of having the conservation of energy, it is advisable that all fonts should either be vertical or tilted right.

WEBVASTU

The solid fonts

There are many types of fonts like solid fonts and hollow fonts. These have to be studied carefully. The solid font gives a heavy look and thus should only be placed in South-west and never in North/ North-east/ East. Similarly, the hollow font gives a very light look and should always be placed in North/East/North-east quadrant and never in South/West/South-west side.

WEBVASTU WEBVASTU

7.9 Graphics As Per Vastu

The graphics should be placed in a rhythmic manner and there should be a flowing feeling. The graphics should not be clustered at one portion.

7.9.1 The Shape

The shape of the graphic is very important as the stability depends on the shape.

Generally square and rectangular shapes are preferred but the shapes, which are narrower at top and broader at base, are very stable. All irregular shapes should be avoided. The shapes such as square, rectangle, circle are stable while the irregular shapes and shapes like triangle, pentagon are not advisable.

The stable shapes are:

The unstable shapes are:

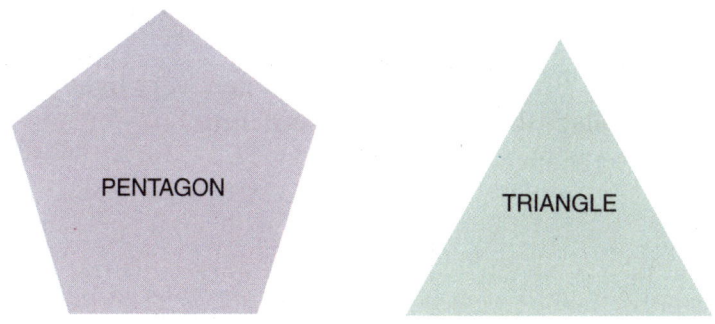

The shapes that are broader at base and narrower at top are stable than those narrower at base and broader at top as the centre of gravity of a cone is $1/3^{rd}$ to that of the square, thus stability is more.

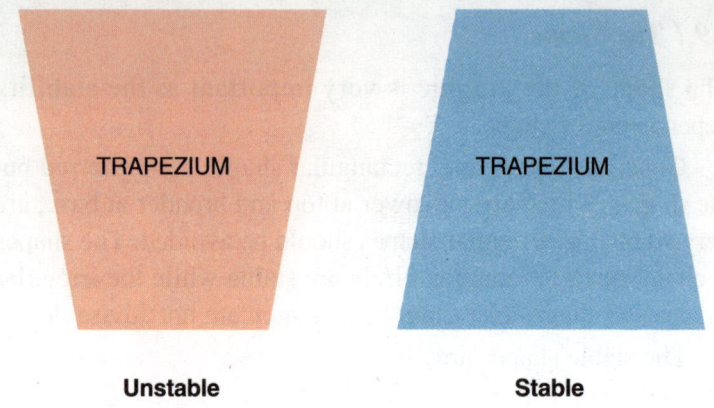

Unstable   Stable

7.9.2 The Placement

The placement of the graphics plays the most important role as it is the thing that decides the heaviness of a particular direction.

- ❖ The heavy graphics should be placed in the South/West/South-west portions.
- ❖ The North/East/North-east should not be overloaded with the graphics and light photos should be placed here.
- ❖ The Brahmasthaan should be kept very light and no collage should be concentrated there.

8 RESEARCH ON THE PROPOSED HTML: THE AIR ELEMENT

HTML is one of the most important things that one must know if one wants to create his/her own personal Web page. It is the language in which all Web pages on the Internet are based and in order to create anything you must know it. This language is a series of letters that are abbreviations of what they actually stand for.

8.1 What is HTML?

HTML is an initial that stands for Hyper Text Markup Language. The Hyper Text Markup Language (HTML) is composed of a set of elements that define a document and guide its display. The break up form is this:

```
<HTML>

  <HEAD>
    <TITLE></TITLE>
  </HEAD>

  <BODY>
  </BODY>
</HTML>
```

Hyper is the opposite of linear. Earlier computer programs had to move in a linear fashion. HTML does not hold to that pattern and allows the person viewing the World Wide Web page to go anywhere, any time they want.

Text is what one uses. Real, honest to goodness English letters.

Mark up is what one does. You will write in plain English and then mark up what you wrote. More to come on that in the next primer.

Language because they needed something that started with 'L' to finish HTML.

8.2 HTML Flags

HTML works in a very simple, very logical, format. It reads from top to bottom, left to right. That's important to remember. HTML is written with TEXT. What you use to set certain sections apart as bigger text, smaller text, bold text, underlined text, is a series of flags. Flags are often understood as commands. For e.g., you want a line of text to be bold. You will put a flag at the exact point you want the bold lettering to start and another flag where you want the bold lettering to stop.

8.2.1 Flag Format

All flag formats are the same. They begin with a less-than sign: < and end with a greater-than sign: >. Always. No exceptions. What goes inside the < and > is the flag. Learning HTML is learning the flag to perform whatever command you want to do.

An HTML element may include a name, some attributes and some text or hypertext, and will appear in an HTML document as:

   <tag_name> text </tag_name>

   <tag_name attribute_name=argument> text </tag_name>, or just

   <tag_name>

For example:

   <title> My Useful Document </title>

and

   <a href="argument"> text </a>

An HTML document is composed of a single element:

<html>... </html>

that is, in turn, composed of head and body elements:

<head>... </head>

and

<body>... </body>

To allow older HTML documents to remain readable, <html>, <head>, and <body> are actually optional within HTML documents.

8.2.2 Elements Usually Placed in the Head Element

<title>... </title>

It specifies a document title. It will usually appear in a window bar identifying the contents of the window.

<meta>... </meta>

It specifies the document's keywords and/or descriptions of that particular document, which help in the promotion.

<script>... </script>

This tag helps in calling in external script files which has variable roles to play.

8.2.3 Elements Usually Placed in the Body Element

The following sections describe elements that can be used in the body of the document.

Text Elements

<P> This stands for paragraph. It does the exact same thing as the <BR> above except this flag skips a line. BR just jumps to the next line, P skips a line before starting the text again.

<p>

The end of a paragraph that will be formatted before it is displayed on the screen.

<HR> This command gives you a line across the page. (**HR** stands for Horizontal Reference.) The line right above the words "Single Flags" was made using an <HR> flag.

 This breaks the text and starts it again on the next line. Remember you saved your document as TEXT so where you hit ENTER to jump to the next line was not saved. In an HTML document, you need to denote where you want every carriage return with a <BR>.

Headers

<h1>... </h1> Most prominent header
<h2>... </h2>
<h3>... </h3>
<h4>... </h4>
<h5>... </h5>
<h6>... </h6> Least prominent header

Logical Styles

...
Emphasis
...
Stronger emphasis

Physical Styles

...

Boldface

...

Italics

<u>... </u>

Underline

<tt>... </tt>

8.3 HTML according to Vastu

This is the air element so the slightest change in one of the property will change the whole layout and thus the whole Vastu of the website.

Research on the Proposed HTML: The Air Element 85

For example, this is one of the element of web design and any change in any of the property of the HTML changes the whole look and feel of the design and can adverse the principles of Vastu.

```
<HEAD>
  <TITLE></TITLE>
</HEAD>

<BODY LEFTMARGIN="0" TOPMARGIN="0"><TABLE BGCOLOR="#D9ECFF" WIDTH="100%"
  BORDER="0">
    <TR>
      <TD><BR><BR><BR><BR></TD>
    </TR>
  </TABLE><TABLE BGCOLOR="#BB5E00" WIDTH="150" BORDER="0" HEIGHT="400"
    ALIGN="LEFT">
    <TR>
      <TD><BR></TD>
    </TR>
  </TABLE>
</BODY>
</HTML>
```

This site is in harmony with the Vastu principles as all the graphics and the text is left aligned. The change in one of the small property of table has changed the whole look and feel of the site and the whole principles of Vastu are being adverse.

The simple change of property from left to right has changed the whole layout of the website and the Vastu is changed.

```
<HEAD>
  <TITLE></TITLE>
</HEAD>

<BODY LEFTMARGIN="0" TOPMARGIN="0"><TABLE BGCOLOR="#D9ECFF" WIDTH="100%"
  BORDER="0">
    <TR>
      <TD><BR><BR><BR><BR></TD>
    </TR>
  </TABLE><TABLE BGCOLOR="#BB5E00" WIDTH="150" BORDER="0" HEIGHT="400"
    ALIGN="RIGHT">
    <TR>
      <TD><BR></TD>
    </TR>
  </TABLE>
</BODY>
</HTML>
```

86 *Designing Websites*

Another example is that here the top table has occupied 100% width, thus North and North-east are heavy.

```
<HTML>
<HEAD>
<TITLE></TITLE>
</HEAD>
<BODY LEFTMARGIN="0" TOPMARGIN="0">
<TABLE WIDTH="100%" BORDER="0" CELLPADDING="0" CELLSPACING="0" HEIGHT="130">
<TR>
<TD BGCOLOR="#FF8000">andnbsp;</TD>
```

```
</TR>
</TABLE>
<TABLE WIDTH="150" BORDER="0" CELLPADDING="0" CELLSPACING="0" HEIGHT="480"
ALIGN="LEFT" BGCOLOR="#FF8000">
<TR>
```

```
<TD>andnbsp;</TD>
</TR>
</TABLE>
</BODY>
</HTML>
```

Simply by changing the width the table now occupies only the 50% of the visible area by which making the top right empty implies the North and North-east empty, thus following the Vastu principles.

```
<HTML>
<HEAD>
<TITLE></TITLE>
</HEAD>
<BODY LEFTMARGIN="0" TOPMARGIN="0">
<TABLE WIDTH=" 50%" BORDER=" 0" CELLPADDING ="0" CELLSPA CING ="0" HEIGHT="130">
<TR>
<TD BGCOLOR = "#FF8000">
andnbsp;
</TD>
</TR>
</TABLE>
< T A B L E WIDTH="150" BORDER="0" CELLPADDING="0" CELLSPACING="0" HEIGHT="480" ALIGN="LEFT" BGCOLOR="#FF8000">
<TR>
<TD>andnbsp;</TD>
```

```
</TR>
</TABLE>
</BODY>
</HTML>
```

Here is another example where if we don't assign any value to "VALIGN", the image comes in the middle of the left table. As we change it either "TOP" or "BOTTOM", the image changes its positions respectively. By assigning the value to "Bottom", the image moves to the bottom left of the table and the South-west of the page becomes heavier.

```
<HTML>
<HEAD>
<TITLE></TITLE>
</HEAD>
<BODY LEFTMARGIN="0" TOPMARGIN="0">
<TABLE WIDTH="100%" BORDER="0" HEIGHT="100" CELLPADDING="0" CELLSPACING="0">
<TR>
<TD BGCOLOR="#C0C0C0">andnbsp;</TD>
</TR>
</TABLE>
<TABLE WIDTH="150" BORDER="0" HEIGHT="480" CELLPADDING="0" CELLSPACING="0">
<TR>
<TD BGCOLOR="#C0C0C0"><IMG SRC="stairs.jpg" WIDTH="220" HEIGHT="145"></TD>
</TR>
</TABLE>
</BODY>
</HTML>
```

Research on the Proposed HTML: The Air Element

<HTML>
<HEAD>
<TITLE></TITLE>
</HEAD>
<BODY LEFTMARGIN="0" TOPMARGIN="0">
<TABLE WIDTH="100%" BORDER="0" HEIGHT="100" CELLPADDING="0" CELLSPACING="0">
<TR>
<TD BGCOLOR="#C0C0C0">andnbsp;</TD>
</TR>
</TABLE>
<TABLE WIDTH="150" BORDER="0" HEIGHT="480" CELLPADDING="0" CELLSPACING="0">
<TR>
<TD BGCOLOR="#C0C0C0" VALIGN="TOP"><IMG SRC="stairs.jpg" WIDTH="220" HEIGHT="145"></TD>
</TR>
</TABLE>

</BODY>
</HTML>
<HTML>
<HEAD>
<TITLE></TITLE>

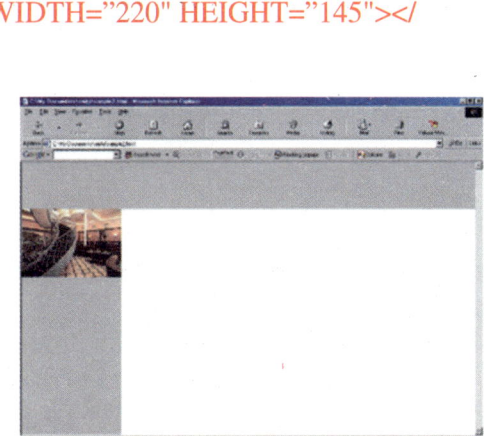

</HEAD>
<BODY LEFTMARGIN="0" TOPMARGIN="0">
<TABLE WIDTH="100%" BORDER="0" HEIGHT="100" CELLPADDING="0" CELLSPACING="0">
<TR>
<TD BGCOLOR="#C0C0C0">andnbsp;</TD>
</TR>
</TABLE>
<TABLE WIDTH="150" BORDER="0" HEIGHT="480" CELLPADDING="0" CELLSPACING="0">
<TR>
<TD BGCOLOR="#C0C0C0" VALIGN="BOTTOM"><IMG SRC="stairs.jpg" WIDTH="220" HEIGHT="145"></TD>
</TR>
</TABLE>
</BODY>
</HTML>

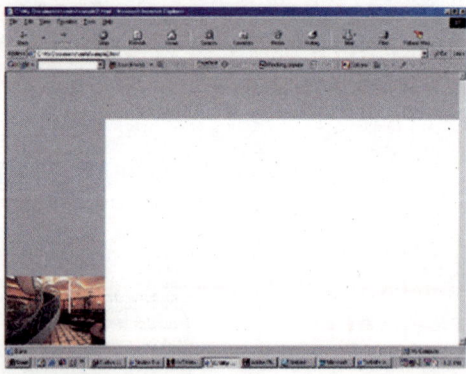

Thus by simply changing a simple property of the HTML, it can create a huge difference and can change the concepts wholly.

9. RESEARCH ON THE PROPOSED COLOURS: THE FIRE ELEMENT

9.1 What is Colour?

A colour is the most powerful decorating element in our lives. Everything comprises colour. Even a light ray is a spectrum of seven colours. An understanding of colour can really help us achieve the goal of a pleasant, personal and comfortable design. Those of us blessed with vision can barely imagine a world without colour. Colours evoke feelings, and stand to represent ideas, and so, in web design, as in all things designed, knowledgeable and appropriate use of colour is critical.

9.2 The Colour Theory

Colour theory encompasses a multitude of definitions, concepts and design applications. All the information would fill several encyclopaedias. As an introduction, here are a few basic concepts. Sir Isaac Newton developed the first circular diagram of colours in 1666. If we understand the basics of the colour, then we can make a perfect colour scheme. The colours are divided into three categories.

9.2.1 Primary Colours

The primary colours were determined in 1861 by Scottish physicist Sir James Clerk-Maxwell. These are the three basic hues – red, blue and yellow. They are the foundation of the colour wheel and all other colours are derived from them. All colours are made from a combination of black, white, and primary colours. Primary colours cannot be created by mixing other colours.

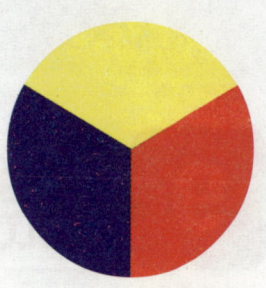

9.2.2 Secondary Colours

When two primary colours are mixed, they form a secondary colour. They are orange, green and violet. Their hues are halfway between the primary colours used to make them.

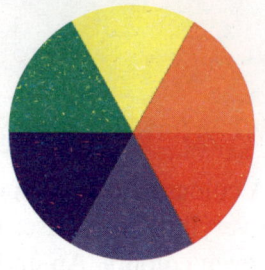

9.2.3 Tertiary Colours

They are created by combining a primary colour with an adjacent secondary colour. There are six tertiary colours (two for each primary colour). They are yellow orange, orange red, red purple, blue purple, blue green, and yellow green. Each of these colours is located on the colour wheel between the primary and secondary colours which are used to make them.

9.2.4 Intermediate Colours

Besides tertiary colours, additional intermediate colours can be added to the colour wheel until it includes a complete spectrum of colours.

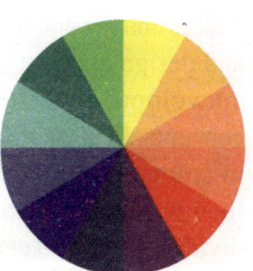

9.3 The Colour Wheel

The colour wheel is a complete picture of all the colours available, once you understand this, there will not be any problem in forming any colour scheme. In the colour

Research on the Proposed Colours: The Fire Element   93

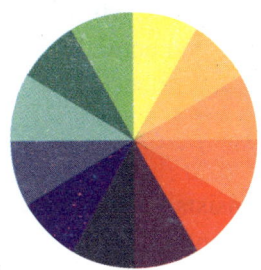

wheel at the right, the primaries form a triangle with equal sides with in the circle, and the secondary forms another triangle opposite to that. Each colour has a 'complement', which is located directly across from it on the wheel. Thus, green is complement of red and orange is complement of blue.

9.4 The Behaviour of Colours

Colours behave in different ways. It is up to us to use their particular behaviour according to our needs. If you remember the basics between these three actions, you can decorate and dress for success.

9.4.1 Active Colours

Active colours are warm colours, they create a feeling of warmth and coziness in a room e.g. yellow, orange and red. These colours inspire positiveness and exude confidence from extroverts. Warm colours can also inspire conversation and upbeat attitudes. Red heats up a room like no other hue.

9.4.2 Passive Colours

Passive colours are cool colours, which pacify and restore. They make an environment cool and serene. In rooms where there's plenty of sunshine, cool colours can provide a calming ambience. Bedrooms, private areas and bathrooms are great places for blues, greens and purples. Other cool colours, such as blues and greens, can evoke quiet moods and even sadness. For this reason, cool colours aren't generally used in large areas.

9.4.3 Neutral Colours

They do not activate or pacify. Instead, they work together with the other colours to bridge rooms and provide transition. Think of neutralising colours as 'uncolours'. Beige, greys, whites and taupe are the best examples. Neutral colours can actually "de-stress" individuals.

9.5 Colour Scheme

A colour scheme for a website usually consists of one or two principal or foundation colours and an accent colour or two. Harmony can be defined as a pleasing arrangement of parts, whether it is music, poetry, and colour. When something is not harmonious, it's either boring or chaotic. Here are a few methods of selecting colour schemes that will enhance your site design.

9.5.1 Analogous Colours

Analogous colours are also called the related colours. They are any three colours, which are adjacent to each other on a 12-part colour wheel, such as yellow-green, yellow, and yellow-orange. Usually one of the three colours predominates. They are essentially colours of a one hue but with varying tints and shades. Related colours are considered to be harmonious. This site is a perfect example of analogous colour. How the shades are used in a rhythm.

9.5.2 Complementary Colours

Complementary colours are any two colours located opposite each other on the colour wheel such as red and green, red-purple, yellow-green. Complementary colours used together make each colour appear more vivid. These opposing colours create maximum contrast and maximum stability. These two sites are showing the use of complementary colours. In the first site, there is a beautiful use of the reds and greens in the muted tones. Other site is a composition with purple and green.

9.5.3 Triad Colours

Another method of selecting colours that will work well together is the triad approach. If you were to use an equilateral triangle as a pointer and spin it within the wheel, each of the three colours pointed to will be harmonious when used together.

9.5.4 Monochromatic Colour Scheme

This colour scheme takes use of black and one other colour. These are two different sites with the use of mono colour with black. In the first site, yellow is used with black and in the other combination of reddish brown and black is there.

9.5.5 Graduation Colour Scheme

It is somewhat related to monochromatic colour schemes which happens when colours are chosen in an order of hue, saturation or lightness.

9.5.6 Contrast Colour Scheme

They are the colour choices that are in opposites with each other in terms of hue, lightness or saturation.

There are other terms that should be taken care of:

Value

The range from black to white is called value.

Contrast

It is the degree of separation between values.

Brightness

It adds white to an image. The lack of brightness tones the image.

Saturation

It is the measurement of colour intensity.

9.6 Colour Symbolism

Colour is a powerful component of design. It effects mood and emotion. It evokes associations with time and place. Colour plays a vitally important role in the world in which we live. Colour can sway thinking, change actions, and cause reactions. It can irritate or soothe your eyes, raise your blood pressure or suppress your appetite. When used in a right way, colour can save on energy consumption. When used in a wrong way, colour can contribute to global pollution. Every colour symbolises a particular character.

9.6.1 State of the Mind

A colour tells directly the mood of the person. Colours do affect our actions and reactions. Colours can create conditions that can cause fatigue, increase stress, decrease visual perception, damage eyesight, increase possible worker errors, and negatively affect orientation and safety. Scientists, doctors and mental health professionals have been studying the correlation between colour and mood for years. Many now believe that colours cannot only cause emotional reactions, but can also correct mood and well-being.

9.6.2 Age of the Person

The colour preferences of adults are always influenced by learned responses and are usually more conservative than those of younger people. Most children like bright, happy colours. Most adults like dull and light colours, Grey is one colour that represents intellectuality and stability.

9.6.3 Culture and the Trend

There are cycles of colour popularity. We learn colour associations from the culture in which we live. Colour symbolism can vary dramatically between cultures. For e.g. Red. Different cultures have their own perceptions for the same colour.

China – symbol of celebration and luck, used in many cultural ceremonies that range from funerals to weddings.

India – colour of purity (used in wedding outfits).

Western cultures – Christmas colour when combined with green; Valentines Day when combined with pink; indicates stop.

Eastern cultures – signifies joy when combined with white.

9.7 Colour Significance

Clever use of colour and good arrangement shows how pictures of very different moods and disparate possessions can be grouped together to make a very satisfactory design. But every colour has its own significance and its own meaning. Here are some of the colours with their effects and the nature they depict.

RED

Red is the most dramatic, emotional and active of the three primaries. It is the hottest of all colours, and as such, represents all things intense and passionate. It is an especially versatile colour in its effects, giving warmth and elegance. It represents heat and fire, speed and zest, blood and excitement, competition and aggression. The use of red suggests a bold and confident attitude. It is used in those areas where one needs excitement like bars. Red is also said to stimulate and symbolise passion.

It can be an irritating, restless colour though, and should only be used when you wish to ignite your visitors. Red makes an excellent accent colour, particularly when used with neutral colours, but clashes with green, blue and purple.

BLUE

Blue is the only colour, which is the most universally equated with the beauty. Blue is timeless, linking the present with tradition and lasting values. It is the most popular colour conveying peace and tranquillity, harmony, trust and confidence. It is the most versatile in expressive values. Psychologically, blue is associated with tranquillity and contentment. It is an excellent complement to earth tones and neutral colours like grey and beige. But be careful when using orange with blue, because these two colours vibrate against each other and cause a jarring effect.

Lighter shades of blue, both solid and textured, make excellent backgrounds for websites which are lighthearted and positive. On the other hand, blue is the worst possible choice when developing sites for food or cooking because there are very few blue foods on earth and it is known to be an appetite suppressant!

YELLOW

It is a powerful colour, both light in value and extremely intense in its purest form. It evokes a sense of energy and excitement. Yellow is a perennial favourite in designing, combining with greens to provide the natural freshness and with red for gaiety and richness.

Yellow signifies optimism, happiness, idealism, and imagination. It conveys bright, cheery feelings in your visitors. If you should decide to use yellow a lot in your site, it works well as a background colour for easy readability with contrasting colours. It is the colour of cleanliness and purity, youth, simplicity and innocence.

Therapists often use colours with the yellow scheme to boost mood. You can achieve the same effect by adding yellows to rooms, which are not associated with happy thoughts, such as kitchens, and laundry rooms. Yellows can also be used to increase energy.

GREEN

Green is the most common choice of the designers. It is a very refreshing colour and often used as a dominant colour. Green goes with every other colour and makes it a natural neutral. It represents the greenery of the nature and thus provides the design with liveliness.

It is a colour that should be used with care, because it generates a strong feeling of either positivity or negativity in most people. But keep in mind that for many people it conjures up imagery of envy, reptiles and insects. If you use green do not closely combine red with green, as these two colours vibrate against each other and make readability nearly impossible, as well as being difficult for the colour blind to read.

VIOLET

It seems to be a colour of emotional contrasts. Its paler tints are unabashedly romantic, fragile and quiet feminine. It enjoyed the popularity in the Victorian era and now as pure colours emerge again. Beautiful violet is certain to be a player.

It is the colour of mystery, royalty and spirituality. For the unconventional and creative, it is not only a good choice, but also often the only choice! When used in a background, as with black, be sure to use a highly contrasting colour for the content so that your words are readable.

ORANGE

It is a warm colour – enthused, vibrant and expansive. It is amazingly versatile, capable of emitting great energy in its purest form and as an earth tone, it evokes warmth, comfort and reassurance. Nowadays, the lighter orange, popularly known as peach is common in use as it gives a cool effect.

If you want to be flamboyant and get attention, use orange! As a predominant colour, however, it can really grate on your visitors nerves, so better to use it sparingly, to highlight certain aspects of your site. Orange would be a poor choice of background colours and combining blues with your orange is a tactful job.

BLACK

It is generally considered a mournful, heavy and depressing colour, but in the right context, can be sophisticated and mysterious. Studies have shown that online reading can be difficult on a black background, but many sites have been done successfully using colours which contrast heavily (white, neon green). Black is the preferred backdrop for an artist's work. In addition, a site, which is highly technical, or has an underground feel, would work well in black.

BROWN

It is another conservative colour, which depicts stability, simplicity, and comfort. It is an earthen colour. Unless it is used correctly, can be very boring. In a site, which depicts the ideas of hearth and home, or outdoor activities. Brown can be a wise choice for graphics.

PASTELS

Pastels are simply lighter tints of any hue. White added to red yields pink and light pink is a pastel. There is not any particular definition for a pastel colour but when colours become so light that they almost seem to be white, they are pastels. The pastels are becoming more and more popular as they create the most sober and elegant look.

NEUTRALS

Using neutrals does not mean not using colour. Any low intensity colour that is used as a background for other accent colours, features, furniture and objects in a space can be classified as neutrals. Neutrals are practical and by changing accessories and fabrics the look of space can be dramatically altered against the same neutral background. For example beige is a neutral colour, which suggests practicality and conservatism. It can be tiresome and plain when alone. It can be used as a background colour with graphics which are earthy, like browns and greens, or blue and pink palettes. Beige is a good colour to use in the background, as it will allow for maximum readability of content. Another example is grey. It is the most conservative of neutral shades, and represents practicality, sadness, security and reliability.

9.8 Colours for the Web Design

Colour is a very important feature of a website. One of the most important things to consider when preparing a design is colour, which is the heart of a website. The trick is to find that happy medium where the colours complement each other and make your pages look simply scrumptious. It effects mood and emotion. It evokes associations with time and place. It is an important factor in determining a site's environment.

At the present time, there are only 216 colours that are common to all computers and all web browsers (Each browser sees 256 colours but only 216 of them are common to all web browsers.). By contrast, the human eye can see 10,000,000 colours. If the image contains colours that don't exist, the eyes of the computer / browser try to mix the colour from the 256 colours available. It tries to patch tiny dots of its colours together to make it look like the colour it doesn't have in its vocabulary. This is called dithering.

Website designers should design for the target audience! Use caution when selecting background colour and text colours.

9.8.1 The Concept

The colours chosen solely depend on the kind of profession the site is dealing into. The message of the site is very important. For e.g. if the site is depicting handicrafts products, then one must use the primary colours more to give a life to the site.

9.8.2 The Basics

It is very important that the designer must follow the colour theory and understand how colours complement and interact with each other. An understanding of the colour wheel, primary, secondary, and tertiary colours will help in selecting colours that enhance the design of your site.

9.8.3 The Consistency

There should always be a feeling of constancy in the site, which gives a feeling of space. It should extend throughout the site. The consistency makes a site a place and the user feels as if he is the part of that place.

9.8.4 The Effect

The designer must be very clear about the effect of the colour he is using in design on the user. Colours can make us feel frivolous or sombre. Some colours command our attention, others make us feel tranquil. Every colour scheme has its own significance. Like sepia tones evoke memories of yesteryear. Psychedelic colour combinations take us back to the 60s. Turquoise and yellow combinations or avocado green remind us of the 50s. Bright blues and yellows are reminiscent of sunny summer days. Corporate greys speak of conservatism and black and white of elegance.

9.8.5 The Harmony

There should always be a balance in the colours otherwise the site will look inconsistent. In visual experiences, harmony is something that is pleasing to the eye. It engages the viewer and it creates an inner sense of order, a balance in the visual experience.

9.8.6 Web-safe Colours

To work with colour, there are different attributes you should know about: value, contrast and brightness, and saturation. By mixing hexadecimal tags, and forcing web-safe colours to do your bidding, one can earn one more little edge over a majority of Web pages out there today.

9.9 Colours according to Vastu

Colours offer a way to enhance nearly every aspect of our lives. It improves our mood by stimulating our minds.

Vastu provides vital guidelines to use the different colours in a proper manner so as to derive the maximum benefit from it. Using the colours according to Vastu can change the effectiveness of the site and creating better ambience.

There are three ways in which one can use the colours according to Vastu.

9.9.1. According to the Governing Planet

Vastu suggests for every direction, there is a planet which has its own lord and every planet has its particular colour. Using favourable colours according to the direction specified can yield dynamic results.

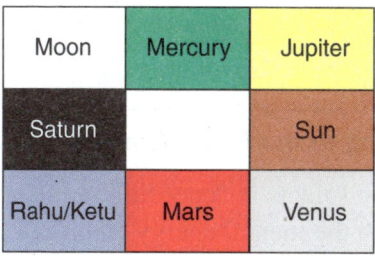

Directions	Planet	Colour Suggested
North	Mercury	Green
Northeast	Jupiter	Yellow
East	Sun	Orange
Southeast	Venus	Silver
South	Mars	Coral Red
Southwest	Rahu/Ketu	Grey Blueish
West	Saturn	Black
Northwest	Moon	White

9.9.2 According to the Zodiac Sign

Colours can be used according to *raashi* or the zodiac sign of the owner.

Zodiac Sign	Colour Suggested
Aries (*Mesh*)	Coral red
Taurus (*Rishab*)	Milky white
Gemini (*Mithun*)	Green
Cancer (*Kark*)	pearl white
Leo (*Sinha*)	Dim white, ruby red
Virgo (*Kanya*)	Different shades of green
Libra (*Tula*)	Cement colour, milky white
Scorpio (*Vrischik*)	Coral red, pink
Sagittarius (*Dhanush*)	Golden yellow
Capricorn (*Makar*)	Dim red, cement colour
Aquarius (*Kumbh*)	Blue, pink
Pisces (*Meen*)	Yellow, sparkling white

9.9.3 According to the Five Elements

The colour one selects is according to the principles one can harmonise with the mental energy and if not, then it will clash with the mood and will make the person irritated. The five

Research on the Proposed Colours: The Fire Element

elements represent a particular colour. All things are made from five element – fire, earth, air, water and sky, and all are colourful. When any thing is unbalanced it is due to colour. And by rectifying that colour you will get correct result. All forces are based on colour. And sun rays also reflect seven colours – blue, green, yellow, orange, red, purple, grey, intra violet and ultra violet. All five elements are represented by some specific colours.

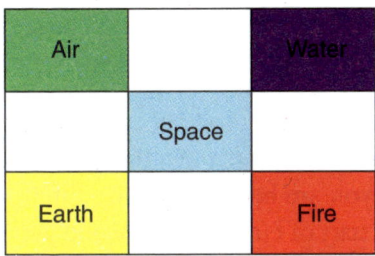

Elements	Colour
Earth	yellow, orange, brown
Water	blue, white
Fire	red, orange
Air	Green
Space	colourless/sky blue

10 RESEARCH ON THE PROPOSED NAMES: THE SPACE ELEMENT

10.1 What is a Name?

A name is the identity of a person, thing or material. This is the word by which you are being recognised in this world. Names are a significant part of culture, family and personal identity, so choosing the right one can seem like a daunting task.

10.2 Hunting a Name

Deciding on a name for your new web page is almost as difficult as deciding what kind of content you want to display. Choosing a name for the site is the most crucial part as by this whole web will know you. This is the first thing when one ever thinks of having a website. Here are some of the points that one should keep in mind while hunting for a name.

10.2.1 The Simplicity

The name should be easy to remember. It should be meaningful and as simple as possible. The name, which is even tough to pronounce, how can, you remember them and then one will avoid those kinds of sites.

10.2.2 The Reflection

A site's name should always reflect the kind of business it is into. It should be descriptive of what your site entails.

For e.g. an interior designer company is called www.sereneinteriors.com. It is easy to recognise and remember. If your site is related to fun, then it should have a funnier name.

10.2.3 The Accessibility

One should always choose a name that will also serve as a keyword for the site so it will show up higher in search engines when people are looking for sites like that.

10.3 Name for the Site

Choosing a name is the first step you take towards establishing a site. A name is the domain name of the site or the URL of the site by which it will make its presence on the web.

10.3.1 The Domain Name

Domains divide worldwide websites into categories based on the nature of the owner and they form part of the site's address or URL i.e., Uniform Resource Locator. Some of the common good domains are:

- *com* for Commercial enterprises
- *org* for Non profit organisations
- *net* for Networks
- *edu* for Educational institutions
- *gov* for Government organisations
- *mil* for Military services
- *int* for Organisations established by International Treaty

10.3.2 The Availability

The availability of a domain name is not always affirmative. If it is available, then one has to get registered but if not then either change the name or try to buy the name you want to. If your first choice is not available keep trying different names until you find one you like that is available.

10.3.3 The Registration

When the domain name is being finalised, then the registration should be a fast process because it is on first come first serve basis. Once the domain name is been registered, then you are the owner of that particular space.

10.3.4 The Hosting

After registration, the next need is the place to host a site. There are various sites, which will host the site free of cost. There are so many of them these days that you may want to look through them first to see who has the best deals.

10.3.5 The Promotion

This is the most deadly consequence of choosing the name. The promotion majority depends on the name of the site, for which the name will be the keyword.

10.4 Name according to Vastu

A name is like the horoscope of the child. Similarly the name of the website is like its horoscope. It has a major effect on the success of the business. The name of the website should be in harmony with the name of the owner.

10.4.1 What are Zodiac signs (Raashis)

The sun is in movement in relation to the earth, though the earth is moving around the earth but the imaginary path of the movement of the sun is called zodiac. The zodiac can be divided into 12 equal parts and in every part group of stars have been recognised. These 12 parts are called *raashis* or zodiac signs. They are:

1. Mesha (Aries)
2. Vrishabh (Taurus)
3. Mithun (Gemini)
4. Kark (Cancer)
5. Sinmha (Leo)
6. Kanya (Virgo)
7. Tula (Libra)
8. Vrishchik (Scorpio)
9. Dhanush (Sagittarius)
10. Makar (Capricorn)
11. Kumbh (Aquarius)
12. Meen (Pisces)

We all know that there are nine planets. There English and Indian names are given below:

Indian Name	English Name
1. Surya	Sun
2. Chandra	Moon
3. Mangal	Mars
4. Budh	Mercury
5. Brahaspati/guru	Jupiter
6. Sukra	Venus
7. Shani	Saturn
8. Rahu	Dragon's head
9. Ketu	Dragons tail

Every *raashi* or zodiac sign is ruled by a planet, which governs the characteristics of that particular zodiac. They are as under:

1. Mesha	Aries	Mars
2. Rishabh	Taurus	Venus
3. Mithun	Gemini	Mercury
4. Kark	Cancer	Moon
5. Sinha	Leo	Sun
6. Kanya	Virgo	Mercury
7. Tula	Libra	Venus
8. Vrishchik	Scorpio	Mars
9. Dhanu	Sagittarius	Jupiter
10. Makar	Capricorn	Saturn
11. Kumbh	Aquarius	Saturn
12. Meen	Pisces	Jupiter

Every person is born under a particular zodiac sign or *raashi* and every zodiac has its own lord and every lord has its enemies and friends.

What exactly I want to say is that the lord of *zodiac* of a person should not be an enemy of the lord of the *zodiac* of the website. For example, my zodiac sign is Saturn, so my website lord should not be Sun or Mars.

Here is the broadly classified table given for the alphabets, which belong to different zodiacs.

Zodiac Sign	Albhabets
Aries (Mesh)	A; L
Taurus (Rishab)	V; U; O
Gemini (Mithun)	K
Cancer (Kark)	H
Leo (Sinha)	M; T
Virgo (Kanya)	P
Libra (Tula)	R
Scorpio (Vrischik)	N
Sagittarius (Dhanush)	Bh
Capricorn (Makar)	J; Kh
Aquarius (Kumbh)	G; S
Pisces (Meen)	D

10.4.2 The Significance of the Numbers

Numbers play a very important role in our science of Web Vastu. It will be in the fitness of things if those numbers are given a weightage, which vibrate with the reduced number of the person owning that website.

For example, if the date of the birth of person owning the website is 8, then emphasis should be laid on 8, 17, 26, 4, 13, 22, 5, 14, 23, 6, 15 and 24.

Now each planet has been assigned a particular number and the number or the website and the owner should be in harmony regarding the planets.

1- Sun   2- Moon
3- Jupiter   4- Rahu
5- Mercury   6- Venus
7- Ketu   8- Saturn
9- Mars

11 THE TIME FACTOR

The time is a very important factor that also determines the success of a website. It plays a very essential role in designing and hosting a site. As in Vastu, before constructing a house, the auspicious time is seek to lay the foundation stone, to start the construction and when the construction is complete, a favourable time is taken care of to move in the house. Similarly in websites, the time of initiation is important and the time of hosting is very important.

Let us discuss some of the basic factors of time.

In the present era, we have developed many types of modern and ultra modern equipments and measuring instruments with the help of which we can have the detailed knowledge of everything. But our saints had written all this 8000 years ago without any appliances but only after their experiences.

11.1 Uttrayan and Dakshinayan

Our earth is tilted at an angle of 23½ degrees on its axis and it completes one circle on its axis in 24 hours approx. This is called the daily movement i.e., the rotation of the earth. Along with it, the earth completes one round of the sun in one year approx. This is the annual movement i.e., the revolution. Rotation of the earth on its axis causes days and nights while revolution around the sun causes changes in seasons and changes the year.

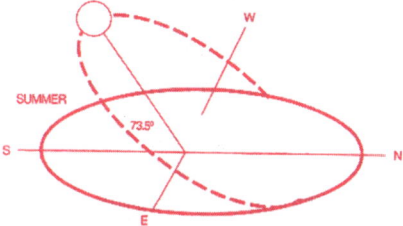

Our earth is divided into two parts, Northern Hemisphere and Southern Hemisphere. On 21st March and 23rd September, the earth takes such a position on its orbit that the rays of the sun fall directly on the equator. During these days, the sunlight falls in both the hemispheres – Northern Hemisphere and Southern Hemisphere equally and day and night are equal everywhere.

After 21st March, the earth moves gradually in such a position that the rays of the sun fall directly and stay longer in the Northern Hemisphere. Therefore days are longer than the nights in the Northern Hemisphere and it is summer season. On 21st June, the rays of the sun fall straight on tropic of cancer. This day is of the longest duration in the Northern Hemisphere and the night is the shortest.

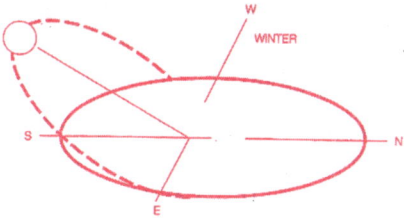

On 23rd September again, day and night are of equal duration. Now the sun shines more directly on the Tropic of Capricorn. The day is of the longest duration and the night is of the shortest duration in the Southern Hemisphere. The summer is in full form is Southern Hemisphere. On the opposite, it is severe winter in the Northern Hemisphere, the night is the longest and the day shortest. From 14th January, the reverse begins gradually.

The period from 14th January to 14th July when the intensity of the sun's rays and its period increases gradually in the Northern Hemisphere is called *Uttrayan* period.

From 14th July to the coming 14th January, the position is just reverse and this period is called *Dakshinayan.* According to Indian astrology, Uttrayan period is auspicious for all kinds of work.

11.2 Shapes of the Moon

The moon is a satellite, which revolves round the earth. The earth itself revolves around the sun along with the moon. The light of the sun is reflected from the moon's surface to us and as a result of it we can see the moon. But positions of the moon, earth and sun keep changing in relation to one another. Therefore, the area of the moon lit by the light of the sun does not remain the same due to various positions of the moon revolving around the earth.

When the moon comes between the earth and the sun, the part of the moon which is away from the earth i.e., which is on the side of the sun, gets light from the sun and as a result we cannot see moon from the earth. This night is called *amavasya* or the moonless night.

On the second day after *amavasya*, the moon that appears in the form of a sharp thin line, this is called new moon. After this, the part of the moon, which appears from the earth, goes on increasing and the period of its appearance also increases. In approximately 14 days, the moon and the sun move in the opposite sides of the earth, and the full-lit moon is seen from the earth. This is called *pooranmaashi* (*Poornima/Poonam*)or full moon night.

After it for the next 15 days, the moon appears full and the part of the moon, which appears from the earth, goes on decreasing and thus it, leads to the position of amavasya. Thus decreasing and increasing phases of the moon as visible from the earth are called the shapes of the moon. When the shape of the moon increases from the new moon (*amavasya*) to the full moon (*poornima*) and the period of visibility goes on increasing daily, the phase is called *Shukla Paksh*. From *poornima* (full moon) to *amavasya* (new moon), when the shape of the moon goes on decreasing daily, it is called *Krishna Paksha*.

11.2.1 Raashis (Zodiac signs)

There are 12 *raashis* as already discussed in chapter 10. Every year the Sun appears in *Mesh* (Aries) at the initial point on approx. April 14 and cross one *raashi* in one month and completes its round of zodiac in one year.

11.2.2 Nakshatras (Constellations)

Nakshatra is a unit of measurement in space. It is an apparent pattern, or grouping, of stars in a region of the sky that man has given a name.

To express the position of the moon in the sky the circular path of the moon is divided into 27 equal parts. Every part is of $13^1/_3$ degrees. Every part has a group of stars which appear in the same relative positions and can be recognised in a form or figure. These 27 parts are called *nakshatras* or constellations. They are as under:

1. Ashwini	2. Bharani	3. Kritika
4. Rohini	5. Mrigashira	6. Ardra
7. Punarvasu	8. Pushya	9. Ashlesh
10. Megha	11. Purva Phalguni	12. Uttar Phalguni
13. Hasta	14. Chita	15. Swati
16. Vishaaka	17. Anuradha	18. Jeshta
19. Moola	20. Purvashada	21. Uttarashada
22. Sravan	23. Dhanishta	24. Satabhisha
25. Purva Bhadrapad	26. Uttar Bhadrapad	27. Revati

Nakshatra can be classified based on qualities like the sex, the location in the sky, the facing, and the nature. While designing the Web Vastu, the auspicious nakshatras are those which rise with their face upwards.

According to learned astrologers, the auspicious time to start anything is in *uttrayan* i.e., between 16th January to 15th July. It means the six months from a year i.e., the *dakshiyanan* period is ruled out. Now Uttrayan covers the month of *Pushya, Magha, Phalguna, Chaitra, Vaishakh, Jaisht* and *Ashaad*. Out of which only three months of *Vaishakh, Pushya* and *Phalgun* are considered auspicious. Hence only three months are left for commencing any construction. Out of this, half, that is one and a half month is ruled out as only *Shukla Paksha* (phase from new moon to full moon) is considered good. Now we have only six weeks available to us for starting anything. Thus, anything that restricts us to work is non-practical. So we should adhere to the auspicious *nakshatras* or *raashis* for deciding the starting of a website and most important while hosting it.

A careful analysis of the main and sub-periods of planets indicate the time of prosperity and adversity in one's life and give us the warning signals to rectify them or to prepare ourselves. This study of planets is also taken care of the favourable times and factors to move ahead with our plans to gain fame, name, money, power and everything.

12 CASE STUDIES

www.sereneinteriors.com

SITE URL:	www.sereneinteriors.com
NATURE OF BUSINESS:	Interior/furniture designing and manufacturing
CONTACT PERSON:	Ms. Smita Jain

Earth

Layout

Page	Layout	North	East	South	West	Bhrmasthan
Home	Good	Light	Light	Light	Light	Light
Inner	Nice	Light	Light	Light	Light	Light

North

Page	Look	Bytes	Colour	Points(10)
Home	Light	2 KB	White, red	8
Inner	Light	Text	Green	6

North-east

Page	Look	Bytes	Colour	Points(10)
Home	Empty	1 KB	White, red	9
Inner	Empty	1 KB	White, red	9

East

Page	Look	Bytes	Colour	Points(10)
Home	Empty	1KB	White	8
Inner	Empty	1 KB	White	8

South-east

Page	Look	Bytes	Colour	Points(10)
Home	Empty	1 KB	White	3
Inner	Empty	1 KB	White	3

South

Page	Look	Bytes	Colour	Points(10)
Home	Text	1 KB	White	1
Inner	Text	1 KB	White	1

South-west

Page	Look	Bytes	Colour	Points(10)
Home	Light	Text	white	1
Inner	Light	Text	White	1

West

Page	Look	Bytes	Colour	Points(10)
Home	Light	2 KB	White, red	1
Inner	Light	2 KB	White, red	1

North-West

Page	Look	Bytes	Colour	Points(10)
Home	Heavy	7 KB	White, red	5
Inner	Heavy	6 KB	White red	5

Bhrmasthaan

Page	Look	Bytes	Colour	Points(10)
Home	Light	Text	White	8
Inner	Light	Text	White	8

Water

Text and Graphics

- Text is ok and has no problems with typography.
- Graphics are not properly balanced, that's why the site is not getting enough money.

Air

HTML Construction

The problem in this site is that the Brahmasthaan is the heaviest, so by just changing a attribute, the collage shifts to left, thus making the Brahmasthaan light and West heavy.

<!DOCTYPE HTML PUBLIC "-//SoftQuad//DTD HoTMetaL PRO 4.0::19970714::extensions to HTML 4.0// EN"

"hmpro4.dtd">

<HTML>
<HEAD>
<TITLE>interior design, home interior, interior designing, interior decor,

interior decorator, vastu shastra, landscaping, furniture designing, layouts, ideal spacing, vastu consultancy, vastu shastra, home plans,

residential projects, commercial projects - Serene Interiors</TITLE>

<META NAME="Keywords" CONTENT="interior design, home interior,vastu consultancy, interior decorator, interior decor, interior designing, interior designer, residential projects, official projects, commerical projects, showrooms, offices, house interior, furniture designing, interior desigining, layouts, vastu shastra, ideal kitchen, ideal spacing, landscaping, serene interiors, indiamart">

<META NAME="Description" CONTENT="Serene Interiors - Indian interior designers providing designs for bedrooms, bathrooms, kitchen, furniture designing, interior decor, houses, residential projects, official projects, commerical projects, showrooms, offices. Vastu Consultancy with weekly vastu articles from vastu shastra expert.">

<META NAME="robots" CONTENT="index,follow">

<META NAME="Author" CONTENT="Raj Kumar Narang, www.indiamart.com">

<LINK HREF="serene-style.css" TYPE="text/css" REL="stylesheet">

<TABLE WIDTH="100%" BORDER="0" CELLPADDING="0" CELLSPACING="0">

<TR>

<TD BACKGROUND="gifs/gr-bg.gif"><IMG SRC="gifs4/serene-interiors-s-btm.gif" ALT="Interior Decoration and Vastu Consultancy" WIDTH="150" HEIGHT="16" BORDER="0">

<TABLE WIDTH="150" BORDER="0" VSPACE="0" HSPACE="0" CELLPADDING="0" CELLSPACING="0" ALIGN="LEFT" BGCOLOR="#737373">

Case Studies

```
<TR>
<TD VALIGN="TOP"><BR>
<BR>
<A HREF="vastu-shastra.html" TARGET=""><!—vimg—>
<IMG SRC="gifs4/vastu-shastra-btn.gif" ALT="Vastu Shastra" WIDTH="150" HEIGHT="16" BORDER="0"></A><BR>
<DIV ALIGN="RIGHT">
<TABLE WIDTH="90%" BORDER="0">
<TR>
<TD CLASS="two"><A HREF="what-is-vastu-shastra.html" TARGET="" CLASS="white">What is Vastu?</A><BR>
<A HREF="history-of-vastu-shastra.html" CLASS="white">History of Vastu</A><BR>
<A HREF="why-vastu-shastra-is-necessary.html" TARGET="" CLASS="white">Why vastu is necessary?</A><BR>
<A HREF="why-vastu-shastra-is-necessary.html#is-vastu-shastra-a-science" CLASS="white">Is Vastu a science?</A><BR>
<A HREF="vastu-shastra-in-21st-century.html" TARGET="" CLASS="white">Vastu in 21st century</A><BR>
<A HREF="vastu-for-humanity.html" TARGET="" CLASS="white">Vastu for humanity</A><BR>
<A HREF="vastu-shastra-articles.html" TARGET="" CLASS="white">Articles on Vastu Shastra</A></TD>
</TR>
```

```
</TABLE></DIV><BR>
<A HREF="dictionaries/index.html" TARGET=""><IMG SRC="gifs4/glossary-btn.gif" ALT="Glossary" WIDTH="150" HEIGHT="16" BORDER="0"></A><BR>
<DIV ALIGN="RIGHT">
<TABLE WIDTH="90%" BORDER="0">
<TR>
<TD><FONT SIZE="-2" FACE="MS Sans Serif, verdana" COLOR="#FFFFFF"><A HREF="dictionaries/vastu-shastra-dictionary.html" TARGET="" CLASS="white">Vastu Dictionary</A><BR>
<A HREF="dictionaries/interior-dictionary.html" TARGET="" CLASS="white">Interior Dictionary</A><BR>
Free Home Planning<BR>
Architectural Dictionary</FONT></TD>
</TR>
</TABLE></DIV><BR>
<A HREF="ideal-spacing.html" TARGET=""><IMG SRC="gifs4/home-planning-btn.gif" ALT="Home Planning" WIDTH="150" HEIGHT="16" BORDER="0"></A><BR>
<DIV ALIGN="RIGHT">
<TABLE WIDTH="90%" BORDER="0">
<TR>
<TD CLASS="two"><A HREF="kitchen.html" TARGET="" CLASS="white">Kitchen</A><BR>
<A HREF="bedroom.html" TARGET="" CLASS="white">Bedroom</A><BR>
<A HREF="bathroom.html" TARGET="" CLASS="white">Bathroom</A></TD>
</TR>
</TABLE></DIV><BR>
```

Fire

Colours

Site Raashi/ Planet	Colour Used	Governing Planet of Business	Colour of Governing Planet	Relation	Colour Suggested
Aquarius-Saturn	White, Green	Venus	Black	Friends	White, black, blue

Space

Name

Site Raashi/ Planet	Owner Name	Owner Raashi/ Planet	Relation
Aquarius-Saturn	Smita	Aquarius -Saturn	Neutral

Time Factor

This site is hosted in *Shukla Paksh*.

Conclusions

- The site is doing an average business and statistics are confirming it.
- Its getting a lot of fame but less money.
- The home page design is South, South-west are empty.
- In the home page, and inner pages, same problems exists.
- The North/North-east are empty.

Suggestions

- The South and the South-west part of the layout should be made heavy.
- The North/North-east are ok.
- The name of the company should be changed.
- The colour scheme should be changed according to any of the principles.

www.vastu-shastra.com

Case Studies   125

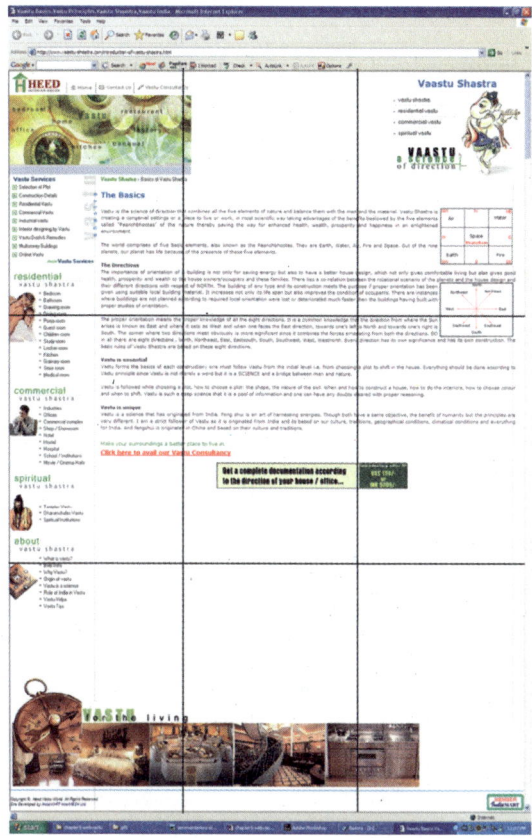

SITE URL:	www.vastu-shastra.com
NATURE OF BUSINESS:	Vastu consultancy
CONTACT PERSON:	Dr. Smita Jain Narang

Earth

Layout

Page	Layout	North	East	South	West	Bhrmasthan
Home	Good	Light	Light	Heaviest	Heavy	Light
Inner	Good	Light	Light	Heaviest	Heavy	Light

North

Page	Look	Bytes	Colour	Points(10)
Home	Light	2 KB	White, green, yellow	9
Inner	Light	1 KB	White	9

North-east

Page	Look	Bytes	Colour	Points(10)
Home	Light	4 KB	White	9
Inner	Light	4 KB	White	9

East

Page	Look	Bytes	Colour	Points(10)
Home	Light	2 KB	White	8
Inner	Empty	Text	White	9

South-east

Page	Look	Bytes	Colour	Points(10)
Home	Heavy	12KB	White, brown	7
Inner	Light	5 KB	White, brown	4

South

Page	Look	Bytes	Colour	Points(10)
Home	Very Heavy	16 KB	Browns	9
Inner	Heavy	12 KB	Browns	8

South-west

Page	Look	Bytes	Colour	Points(10)
Home	Very Heavy	16 KB	Browns	9
Inner	Heavy	12 KB	Browns	8

West

Page	Look	Bytes	Colour	Points(10)
Home	Heavy	8 KB	Browns	8
Inner	Light	2 KB	White	2

North-west

Page	Look	Bytes	Colour	Points(10)
Home	Heavy	9 KB	Green, yellow	7
Inner	Heavy	9 KB	Green, yellow	7

Brahmasthaan

Page	Look	Bytes	Colour	Points(10)
Home	Light	Text	White	9
Inner	Light	Text	White	9

Water

Text and Graphics

❖ Text is fine and has no problems with typography.
❖ Graphics are properly balanced, that's why the site is getting enough query.

Air

HTML Construction

There is no as such problem and this is almost designer according to Vastu.

<!DOCTYPE HTML PUBLIC "-//SoftQuad//DTD HoTMetaL PRO 4.0::19971010::extensions to HTML 4.0//EN"
"hmpro4.dtd">

```
<HTML>
<TABLE WIDTH="100%" BORDER="0" CELLSPACING="0" CELLPADDING="0" HSPACE="0" VSPACE="0">
<TR>
<TD WIDTH="100%"><IMG SRC="gifs/vastu-shastra-head.jpg" ALT="Vastu - Vastu Shastra,Vastu Consultant,Indian Vastu,Indian Vastu Shastra" BORDER="0" WIDTH="455" HEIGHT="190"></TD>
<TD WIDTH="171" BACKGROUND="gifs/ganpatimukut.gif" VALIGN="TOP"><IMG SRC="gifs/zero.gif" WIDTH="171" HEIGHT="1" BORDER="0"><BR>
<DIV CLASS="toplnk"><IMG SRC="gifs/arrow.gif" WIDTH="6" HEIGHT="5" BORDER="0" HSPACE="6"><A HREF="vastu-shastra.html">vastu shastra</A><BR>
<IMG SRC="gifs/dotted-line.gif" WIDTH="171" HEIGHT="10" BORDER="0"><BR>
<IMG SRC="gifs/arrow.gif" WIDTH="6" HEIGHT="5" BORDER="0" HSPACE="6"><A HREF="residential-vastu.html">residential vastu</A><BR>
<IMG SRC="gifs/dotted-line.gif" WIDTH="171" HEIGHT="10" BORDER="0"><BR>
<IMG SRC="gifs/arrow.gif" WIDTH="6" HEIGHT="5" BORDER="0" HSPACE="6"><A HREF="commercial-vastu.html">commercial vastu</A><BR>
<IMG SRC="gifs/dotted-line.gif" WIDTH="171" HEIGHT="10" BORDER="0"><BR>
<IMG SRC="gifs/arrow.gif" WIDTH="6" HEIGHT="5"
```

BORDER="0" HSPACE="6"><A HREF="spiritual-vastu.html">spiritual vastu</A></DIV>
<IMG SRC="gifs/zero.gif" WIDTH="1" HEIGHT="9">
<IMG SRC="gifs/vastu-a-science.gif" ALT="Vastu a Science" BORDER="0" WIDTH="171" HEIGHT="67"></TD>
<TD WIDTH="154" BACKGROUND="gifs/ganpati-mukut.gif" ALIGN="CENTER" VALIGN="TOP"><IMG SRC="gifs/lord-ganpati.jpg" ALT="Lord Ganesha" BORDER="0" WIDTH="154" HEIGHT="190"></TD>
</TR>
</TABLE>
<TABLE WIDTH="100%" BORDER="0" CELLPADDING="0" CELLSPACING="0">
<TR>
<TD WIDTH="165" VALIGN="TOP" BACKGROUND="gifs/lft-tbl-bg.gif"><IMG SRC="gifs/zero.gif" WIDTH="165" HEIGHT="1" BORDER="0">
<DIV CLASS="lft-hd"><A HREF="vastu-services.html"><B>Vastu Services</B></A></DIV>
<DIV CLASS="lft-links"><A HREF="vastu-for-selection-of-plot.html">Selection of Plot</A>
<A HREF="vastu-for-construction-details.html">Construction Details</A>
<A HREF="residential-vastu.html">Residential Vastu</A>
<A HREF="commercial-vastu.html">Commercial Vastu</A>

```
<A HREF="vastu-for-industry.html">Industrial vastu</A><BR>
<A HREF="interior-design-according-to-vastu.html">Interior designing by Vastu</A><BR>
<A HREF="vastu-remedies.html">Vastu Dosh andamp; Remedies</A><BR>
<A HREF="vastu-for-multistoried-buildings.html">Multistorey Buildings</A><BR>
<A HREF="vastu-online.html">Online Vastu</A></DIV>
<DIV ALIGN="RIGHT" CLASS="more">...more <B><A HREF="vastu-services.html">Vastu Services</A></B></DIV> </TD>
<TD ALIGN="CENTER">
<TABLE WIDTH="280" BORDER="0" CELLPADDING ="0" CELLSPACING="0">
<TR>
<TD><A HREF="residential-vastu.html"><IMG SRC="gifs/residential-vastu-tlt.gif" ALT="Residential Vastu" WIDTH="202" HEIGHT="59" BORDER="0"></A></TD>
<TD><IMG SRC="gifs/compass-tlt.jpg" ALT="Compass" WIDTH="78" HEIGHT="59" BORDER="0"></TD>
</TR>
</TABLE>
<TABLE WIDTH="280" BORDER="0" CELLPADDING ="0" CELLSPACING="0">
<TR>
<TD WIDTH="107" VALIGN="TOP" BACKGROUND=" gifs/line-bg-hm.gif"><A HREF="
```

residential-vastu.html"> <IMG SRC="gifs/family.jpg" ALT="Family" WIDTH="107" HEIGHT="117" BORDER="0"></A></TD>
<TD WIDTH="100%" BACKGROUND="gifs/compass-bg.jpg"><IMG SRC="gifs/zero.gif" WIDTH="173" HEIGHT="1" BORDER="0">
<DIV CLASS="lnks2"><A HREF="vastu-for-bedroom.html" >Bedroom</A>
<A HREF="vastu-for-bathroom.html">Bathroom</A>
<A HREF="vastu-for-drawing-room.html">Drawing room</A>
<A HREF="vastu-for-dining-room.html">Dining room</A>
<A HREF="vastu-for-pooja-room.html">Pooja room</A>
<A HREF="vastu-for-guest-room.html">Guest room</A>
<A HREF="vastu-for-children-room.html">Children room</A>
<A HREF="vastu-for-study-room.html">Study room</A>
<A HREF="vastu-for-kitchen.html">Kitchen</A></DIV>
<DIV ALIGN="RIGHT" CLASS="more">...<A HREF="residential-vastu.html">more</A>andnbsp;andnbsp;andnbsp;andnbsp;andnbsp;andnbsp;</DIV></TD>
</TR>
</TABLE><IMG SRC="gifs/cat-btm.gif" WIDTH="280" HEIGHT="15" BORDER="0"></TD>
<TD><IMG SRC="gifs/zero.gif" WIDTH="50" HEIGHT="1" BORDER="0"></TD>

```
<TD ALIGN="CENTER" VALIGN="TOP">
<TABLE WIDTH="280" BORDER="0" CELLPADDING ="0" CELLSPACING="0">
<TR>
<TABLE WIDTH="280" BORDER="0" CELLPADDING ="0" CELLSPACING="0">
<TR>
<TD WIDTH="107" VALIGN="TOP" BACKGROUND ="gifs/line-bg-hm.gif"><A HREF="commercial-vastu.html"><IMG SRC="gifs/businessman.jpg" ALT="Businessman" WIDTH="107" HEIGHT="117" BORDER="0"></A></TD>
<TD WIDTH="100%" BACKGROUND="gifs/compass-bg.jpg" VALIGN="TOP"><IMG SRC="gifs/zero.gif" WIDTH="173" HEIGHT="1" BORDER="0">
<DIV CLASS="lnks2"><A HREF="vastu-for-industry.html">Industries</A><BR>
<A HREF="office-vastu.html">Offices</A><BR>
<A HREF="vastu-for-commercial-complex.html">Commercial complex</A><BR>
<A HREF="shop-showroom-vastu.html">Shop / Showroom</A><BR>
<A HREF="vastu-for-hotels.html">Hotel</A><BR>
<A HREF="vastu-for-hostel.html">Hostel</A><BR>
<A HREF="vastu-for-hospital.html">Hospital</A><BR>
<A HREF="vastu-for-institutions.html">School</A> /
<A HREF="vastu-for-institutions.html">Institutions</A><BR>
<A HREF="vastu-for-movie-cinema-halls.html">Movie / Cinema Halls</A></DIV>
</TD>
```

```
</TR>
</TABLE>      <IMG      SRC="gifs/cat-btm.gif"
WIDTH="280" HEIGHT="15" BORDER="0"></TD>
</TR>
</TABLE>
```

Fire

Colours

Site Raashi/ Planet	Colour Used	Governing Planet of Business	Colour of Governing Planet	Relation	Colour Suggested
Mercury	White, green, yellow	Saturn	Black	Friends	White, black, blue

Space

Name

Site Raashi/ Planet	Owner Name	Owner Raashi/ Planet	Relation
Mercury	Smita	Saturn	Friends

Time Factor

This site is hosted in *Shukla Paksh*.

Conclusions

- ❖ The site is doing a good business and statistics are confirming it.
- ❖ Its getting a lot of fame and money.
- ❖ The home page design is empty in North, North-east, Brahmasthaan.
- ❖ The South, South-west and West are very heavy which is very good.
- ❖ In the home page, and inner pages, same things exists.
- ❖ The colour scheme is pretty good.

BIBLIOGRAPHY

B. B. Puri, *Vastu Science for 21st Century*, New Age Books, New Delhi, 2003.

B. B. Puri, *Vedic Architecture and Art of Living*, Vastu Gyan Publication, New Delhi, 1998.

B. B. Puri, *Applied Vastu Shastra in Modern Architecture*, Vastu Gyan Publication, New Delhi, 1997.

N. H. Sahastrabudhe and R. D. Mahatame, *Secrets of Vastu Shastra*, Sterling Paperbacks, New Delhi 1998.

Umed Singh Dugar, *Vastu Rahasya*, B. Jain Publishers Pvt. Ltd., Delhi, 1996.

Gouru Tirupati Reddy, *The Secret of Vastu World*, Prajahita Publishers, Hyderabad, 1994.

Hofstadesti Douglas R., *Meta Magical Themes, Questioning for the Essence of Mind and Pattern*.

Boulding, Kenneth, *The Meaning of the Twentieth Century: The Great Transitions*, New York, 1968.

Sashikala Ananth, *The Penguin Guid to Vastu*, Penguin Books India, New Delhi, 1998.

P. C. Bhatla, *The Gift of Life*, Ritika and Radhika Publications, New Delhi, 1998.

Stapati, Ganapati, *Vastu Shastra*, Vastu Vedic Research Foundation, Madras, 1997.

Cheiro, *Cheiro's Books of Numbers*, Arrow Books Limited, London, 1986.

Schul Bill, Petit (Ed), *The Secret Power of Pyramids*, Random House Inc., New York, 1983.

Prof. V. V. Raman, *Principles and Practice of Vastu Shastra*, Jaipur, 1996.

S. K. Mehta, *Vastu Shastra for prosperity*, Jaipur, 2000.